AL-HALLAJ

CURZON SUFI SERIES
Series Editor:
Ian Richard Netton
*Reader in Arabic and Islamic Civilization and Thought,
University of Exeter*

The *Curzon Sufi Series* attempts to provide short introductions to a variety of facets of the subject, which are accessible both to the general reader and the student and scholar in the field. Each book will be either a synthesis of existing knowledge or a distinct contribution to, and extension of, knowledge of the particular topic. The two major underlying principles of the Series are sound scholarship and readability.

ABDULLAH ANSARI OF HERAT
An Early Sufi Master
A.G. Ravan Farhadi

PERSIAN SUFI POETRY
An Introduction to the Mystical Use of Classical Persian Poetry
J.T.P. de Bruijn

RUZBIHAN BAQLI
Mysticism and the Rhetoric of Sainthood in Persian Sufism
Carl W. Ernst

BEYOND FAITH AND INFIDELITY
The Sufi Poetry and Teachings of Mahmud Shabistari
Leonard Lewisohn

AL-HALLAJ

Herbert W. Mason

CURZON
PRESS

First published in 1995
by Curzon Press
St John's Studios, Church Road, Richmond
Surrey, TW9 2QA

© 1995 Herbert W. Mason

Typeset in Baskerville by Excel Books, New Delhi
Printed in Great Britain by
Biddles Limited, Guildford and King's Lynn

All rights reserved. No part of this book may be reprinted or reproduced or utilised in any form or by any electronic, mechanical, or other means, now known or hereafter invented, including photocopying and recording, or in any information storage or retrieval system, without permission in writing from the publishers.

British Library Cataloguing in Publication Data
A catalogue record for this book is available from the British Library

Library of Congress in Publication Data
A catalog record for this book has been requested

ISBN 0 7007 0311 X

CONTENTS

	Foreword	ix
I.	The Facts of his Life and Theme of Disappearance	1
II.	The Resurfacing of his Life and its Repeated Impact	35
III.	The Problem of Universalism	53
IV.	The Question of Uniqueness	63
V.	Reprise: Who was Hallaj and what is his Place in Islamic Mysticism?	75
VI.	The Death of al-Hallaj	88
VII.	Selected Bibliography	98
	Name Index	103
	Index of Terms	105

Also by Herbert Mason

POETRY

The Death of al-Hallaj, a Dramatic Narrative
Gilgamesh, a Verse Narrative
A Legend of Alexander and *The Merchant and the Parrot, two Dramatic Poems*

FICTION

Gilpins Point, a novella
Summer Light, a novel

MEMOIR

Memoir of a Friend : Louis Massignon
Moments in Passage

STUDIES AND TRANSLATIONS

The Passion of al-Hallaj by Louis Massignon, (4 vols)
Hallaj, Martyr and Mystic by Louis Massignon, 1 vol. abridgement
Testimonies and Reflections
Two Statesmen of Mediaeval Islam
Reflections on the Middle East Crisis

For my friends and colleagues, especially
Salih Altoma, Dino Cavallari, Albert Duclos, Jabra Ibrahim Jabra,
James Langford, George Makdisi, Seyyed Hossein Nasr,
Annemarie Schimmel, Huston Smith, and Merlin Swartz

Transliterations

th	ث
ḥ	ح
kh	خ
dh	ذ
sh	ش
s	ص
d	ض
t	ط
z	ظ
'	ع
gh	غ
q	ق

Persian Consonants

p	پ
ch	چ
g	گ

FOREWORD

"You know and are not known, You see and are not seen."
-*Akhbâr al-Hallâj*, no. 44, 1.4

This is that mysticism in which one is decentered before the unknowable whom one cannot know or imagine or liken anything to : an absolute imageless other who is best likened to nothing in order to preserve one's purity of faith in what one insists is an actual, conscious, deliberate and involving yet transcendent presence. This presence exceeds the collectivity of human presences and faculties for knowing and doing and yet is intimate with it and indeed distinguishes each member from each even as he, traditionally He, perceives and actively involves the whole in His own unknowable reality which is meant to be each one's only center. Is this literally blind faith or delusion of the most extreme sort imaginable? Is this *scientia intuitiva* of the highest order imaginable?

This third/tenth century mystic in the Islamic monotheistic tradition who was nurtured from childhood by the Qur'an and its cited prophets, including Abraham, Moses, Elijah, and Jesus, who studied the sects and denominations to understand them and believed them to be "a single unique principle with numerous expressions," (*Dîwân*, M.L., 1.I) was taken very seriously in his own time to the point of gathering both disciples and enemies throughout the Islamic world and of being regarded as a political threat to the state and being executed in 922 AD for the charge of heresy; and thereafter regarded as a threat to Muslim orthodoxy (Ibn Taymîya, d. 1328 AD;) or as a supreme lover of God (Rûmî, d. 1273 AD;).

Though an ecstatic mystic as the accounts (*akhbâr*) by his contemporaries and his extant poetry and prose indicate, he engaged himself in the most conventional rites of his faith and approached the failings of authorities who abused their positions of power with the highest moral perceptiveness and integrity, and saw the sources of society's evils with clarity as being rooted in human greed and betrayal of religious and humanitarian ideals. All of his rational, critical perceptions were based on the same blind faith in which his God was his entire hearing and his sight, his thought and very breath (*Dîwân*, Q.I).

If it was to nothing he prayed and with nothing he conversed, his life of delusion was a human tragedy of the highest, most terrifying order, in which we who view it from afar through texts and our sense of dramatic verisimilitude share in the terror and yearn with him for the grasp of that

Foreword

ultimate reality that would give his and, with him, our life meaning. He died willingly, to our disbelief and further terror, even joyously, to the point of dancing in his chains as he was led from prison along the Baghdad esplanade to his shocking dismemberment and execution. His story is one of unhinging human self-assurance and spiritual selflessness, one of simplicity unattainable to most of us, in witness of this similitude of nothingness. It remains an awesome mystery and guide across the ages to those who would pursue the truth of our human existence to its deepest and most exacting unfathomable source.

Our current knowledge of this mystic, Husayn ibn Mansûr, of Persian origin, Arabic speaking and writing, born in a village of southwestern Iran in 858 AD, educated in the traditionalist Qur'anic schools of his region and in mysticism and philosophical inquiry in the schools of each developed in Khurasan and in the capital city of Baghdad in the century of his birth, is due largely to the devotion and painstaking research of the late French Islamicist Professeur Louis Massignon (d. 1962) of the Collège de France. Massignon did the pioneering work of collecting, verifying, editing, translating, and analyzing the primary texts, eyewitness accounts, subsequent commentaries on the works and life by Muslims and others down to and including his own time. His work has been criticized, praised, amended, and ideologically disapproved of by several scholars, including former students and others influenced directly or indirectly by his methodology and insights. Notable among the not uncritical continuers of research on Hallaj and other mystics of his time and subsequent to it are Roger Arnaldez, Louis Gardet, Paul Nwyia, Annemarie Schimmel, and Kamil M. ash-Shaibi to name a few among those whose works are listed in the Bibliography of this book. Massignon's magisterial study of the life, teaching, and legacy of the mystic, *La Passion d'al-Hallâj*, was expanded from two volumes in its 1922 Paris edition to four in its posthumous 1975 Paris edition, and is available in English translation through Princeton University Press, 1983, and in abridged form through the same publisher, 1994. Further, his important methodological study of the language of Islamic mysticism, in Paris editions of 1922, 1935, and 1954, has been updated and translated through Notre Dame University Press, 1995. Finally, his shorter seminal studies of Hallaj and Muslim mysticism have been collected and published in three volumes of his *Opera Minora* listed here in the Bibliography.

The textual basis for the present volume consists primarily of the *Akhbâr al-Hallâj*, 3rd edition of Paul Kraus and Louis Massignon, selected poetry from the *Dîwân al-Hallâj*, and the prose *Kitâb at-Tawâsîn* of Hallaj, the latter available in

English translation in full, volume 3 of the Princeton edition. Drawn upon also are numerous other early, precursory and sub-sequent texts of Islamic mysticism, in Arabic and Persian especially, along with commentaries, updates and revisions by more recent Muslim and non-Muslim scholars.

To this is added cautiously the acquaintance with Islamic history, literature and tradition derived from over thirty years of studying and teaching aspects and dimensions of the civilization to which Hallaj belonged and which in his mind his martyrdom reaffirmed.

I

"He will be veiled to my glances until my body disappears (*talâsha*) in the lights of His Essence (*anwârî thâtîhi*); and then no trace, no mark, no aspect and no memory of me will remain."

- *Akhbâr*, no. 10

THE FACTS OF HIS LIFE AND THEME OF DISAPPEARANCE

The facts of his life are this: he was born Husayn ibn Mansûr[1] of Persian parents ca. 244 AH/858 AD in the village of Tur, district of Bayda in the Arabicized province of Fars in south-western Iran. His father, a wool carder (*hallâj*), a profession practised intermittently by his son, followed his trade through such textile centers as Ahwaz and

---

1. His first name, al-Husayn, was given by his father Mansûr, a convert to Islam, his grandfather, Mahammâ, who remained a Zoroastrian, and a surname, Abû 'Abdallâh, completed his names, added to which were those of his place of origin and main residence and of course in his case notable soubriqet; thus, he was Abû 'Abdallâh al-Husayn ibn Mansûr ibn Mahammâ al- Baydâwî al-Baghdâdî al-Hallâj. The *Ta'rîkh Baghdâd* source for this and other facts will be listed in the bibliography.

Tustar, settling his family eventually in the traditionalist Sunnite Arab town of Wasit in southern Iraq ca. 255/868. In 260/873, having completed his basic education in the Hanbalite Qur'anic school of that fervent center, the young Hallaj returned alone to Tustar, where he became a disciple of a celebrated Sunnite Qur'anic scholar and mystic named Sahl, whose approach to the primary source of his Muslim faith was decidedly and decisively for the young apprentice more esoteric and interiorizing than had been the instruction by memorization and exoteric commentary in Wasit. Sahl's path harkened back to and extended the intense detachment from the world of the earliest ascetics of Islam, notably to the Islamic first century's Hasan of Basra, the willfully dark and mournful Persian precursor and indeed spiritual progenitor named in most later mystics' chains of mystical authority (*isnâd*). He remained with Sahl for approximately two years, after which he made his way westward once again to Iraq, this time to Basra in the far south where he made his profession of Sufism and received the Sufi habit, implying commitment to a common rule of life and a carefully prescribed and historically authenticated path.

Basra at the time was a center for the diffusion of the Sufi movement, the principal distinct but corresponding schools having grown up in

The Facts of His Life and Theme of Disappearance

Khurasan in northeastern Iran and in the capital city of Baghdad, where the mystic Muhâsibî (d. 243/857) had moved from Basra with his followers to form that major center whose most eminent shaykh would be Junayd (d. 298/910). In Basra Hallaj came under the direct influence of one close to Junayd, 'Amr Makkî. (d. 297/909)

In 264/877 he married there the daughter of Abû Ya'qûb Aqta', a secretary of Junayd and fellow Sufi of 'Amr Makkî. Of this, his only marriage, there would be three sons and a daughter. One of these sons, Hamd, left an account of his father's later life and martyrdom. According to this account a quarrel between the two Sufis over the marriage, of which 'Amr Makkî disapproved, led Hallaj to journey north to Baghdad to consult Junayd.

Evidence of such spiritual jealousy and possessiveness accompanied Hallaj throughout his life and grew from excessive attachment to him by his masters and, later, disciples, exacerbating any eventual doctrinal differences that arose. Junayd, the recognized leader of the schools of Iraq, advised the cultivation of patience in the spiritual tradition of Hasan of Basra, and Hallaj returned to his life in the home of his father-in-law in Basra.

This town, built originally as a frontier garrison outpost during the rapid expansion period of Islam into Mesopotamia and Iran, following the death of the Prophet Muhammad in 11/632, had become an Arab literary center in the Umayyad period. It was in this post-classical period, that is, between the death of the last of the so-called Rightly Guided Caliphal successors, 'Ali, the Prophet's son-in-law in 41/661, and the emergence of the 'Abbasid dynasty and its successful revolt in 133/750, that the Umayyad Caliph 'Abd al-Malik from his capital in Damascus had defined the conquered regions of Mesopotamia and Iran to the Oxus River in eastern Khurasan as "Al-'Iraq", the two Iraqs, western and eastern, and put them under the governing control of his leading military commander Hajjâj, a near legendary figure of early Islam. This man of cultural grandeur and iron rule commanding first from the garrison towns of Basra and Kufa and eventually building as governor his own capital of Wasit, midway between the two, created an atmosphere through his ostentatious patronage conducive to a flowering of Arabic philological studies and authoritative Qur'anic recitation. Among later Sufis he was remembered most for his failed attempt to compete personally in both "sciences" with the ascetic Hasan of Basra, whom he invited to his palace in Wasit in order to discredit. This was incidentally one of the first confrontations in Islam between a state and a purely spiritual leader over the issue of authority argued as it was on the

The Facts of His Life and Theme of Disappearance   5

plane of Arabic and Qur'anic knowledge. Such confrontation would become a recurring theme in Islamic history with variations in argument centered on the same unsettled issue. Basra, however, gradually yielded its prominent position in the later Umayyad and early 'Abbasid period to its northern sister outpost Kufa and ultimately to Baghdad as a center of Arabic grammatical and philological and Qur'anic studies. The Basra sojourn influenced Hallaj in two principle ways: the imprint upon his language of mystical thought and, from its older Arabic heritage, styles of didactic and lyric poetry; and the quickening of his consciousness of social injustice.

Basra had become in the third Islamic century a center also of social crisis, prompted by the revolt of black slaves, the Zanj, imported from the Sudan and East Africa to dig in the salt mines of lower Iraq. As a result of gross mistreatment by the 'Abbasid Sunnite masters ruling from Baghdad and aroused by opposition from Shi'ite propagandists using the issue to undermine the authority of the dynasty's central government, the banner was raised as an outcry for justice in a religious community that professed equality among all members. It was a classic confrontation between the major sectarian divisions also derived from early Islamic history; and Hallaj found himself in the middle of the crisis through his Shi'ite in-laws, the Karnabâ'î family, who supported the revolt ideologically.

Hallaj, a Sunnite of a strong traditionalist formation, found himself in a Shi'ite milieu, one that had been deeply imbued with Hellenistic and neo-gnostic cultural attitudes and thought throughout the century of his birth, the century that saw the founding of the famous *Bayt al-hikma* translation center in Baghdad for the dissemination of Greek learning and ideas under the patronage of the quasi-Shi'ite, anti-traditionalist Caliph al-Ma'mûn. Most important for Hallaj and other traditionalist Sufis would be the influence of a philosophical vocabulary and a dialectic mode upon their Sunnite response to Shi'ite propaganda. His aroused level of dialogue, both on the subject of justice and on the defense of Qur'anic based Islam, was determined in this intense period. Furthermore, his exposure to other religious perspectives and traditions, long a Shi'ite predisposition formed through its concerted intellectual, political, and cultural opposition to Sunnite "orthodoxy", left the apparent imprint of eclecticism upon him and gave rise later among certain of his Sunnite enemies to accusations of his being a Shi'ite or even a Christian in disguise. His identification with the awaited Shi'ite *Mahdi* by certain of his later devotees also led his early

Shi'ite supporters to eventually accuse him of falsehood and assumption of religious prophethood belonging to them. In sum, it was a period that exposed his character to the dangers of spiritual sectarianism, long a feature of Islamic history, and something Hasan of Basra had descried for his Community; and now it helped set the stage for Hallaj's martyrdom, which in his passion for justice and unity of all Muslims under God he appeared to invite.

The Zanj revolt failed in 270/883 and the 'Abbasid Caliph Muwaffaq firmly in power in the capital reestablished control over Basra and the southern region of Iraq. Hallaj soon after made the first of his three extended pilgrimages to Mecca, this on the *'Umra* or minor pilgrimage performable at any time of the year, in this instance remaining there for the duration of one year, during which he was said to fast continuously in preparation for a higher ascetical calling. Like Hasan of Basra and many subsequent Sufis he saw the purification of his own heart as prerequisite for the realization of any moral and spiritual vocation on behalf of his Community. It was most probably this youthful experience that strengthened his conviction of the meaning of the *sayha bi'l-Haqq,* the outcry of justice as witness of the true Reality of God and the Truth of God's transcendent Uniqueness. After it he appears to have become confirmed in his opposition to political extremism and tyranny of any coloration as well as to quietistic Sufism of the sort he ascribed, rightly or wrongly, to his masters, including Junayd, who in his mind represented detachment and withdrawel in prayer from any engagement in political activity. This rejection of quietism separated him thus from the traditional ascetical stance defined originally by Hasan of Basra, who had preached patient endurance in the face of tyranny and the cultivation of fear and sorrow (*khawf wa huzn*); fear in anticipation of God's Judgement and the world to come, and sorrow over our and others' sins in the world in which we find ourselves now.

It was roughly around this period that he engaged in discussions with three notable Sufis that clarified these positions as well as his developing position on personal inspiration from God (*ilhâm*): in Mecca with 'Amr Makkî; in Kufa with Ibrahîm Khawwâs; and in Baghdad with Junayd. Hamd, in his biographical account, mentions a meeting at this time between his father and Junayd with a group of Sufis (*fuqarâ'*) in which a question was posed concerning "the desire for a personal mission (*mudda'î*)" and about which Junayd advised patience and calm to the obviously agitated youth. Other sources place this meeting at the time of the marriage crisis during their first and

The Facts of His Life and Theme of Disappearance 9

possibly, in fact, their only encounter. What matters from all this is his divergence from traditional Sufism as maintained by the Baghdad school. In Basra, however, to which he returned to rejoin his wife following his pious retreat in Mecca, he attracted a number of disciples and commenced his "personal mission".

A year later, his father-in-law renounced him and his positions, and Hallaj left Basra for Tustar with his wife and his brother-in-law, a Karnabâ'î Shi'ite associate, where he preached (in Arabic, as he spoke no Persian) to Arabicized audiences with considerable success. He continued to be attacked in letters sent from Basra by his former master 'Amr Makkî which were instrumental in making him forego for himself any further ties with Sufi masters and the garb of Sufism itself, though this garb remained one of his many "costumes" during his travels on occasion and, later, in prison in Baghdad.

Once returned to his familiar Islamized and Arabicized Iranian cultural milieu, around the centers of Tustar and Ahwaz, he became a visitor in the circles of landed gentry, upper echelon bureaucrats, and well-to-do patrons, the so-called *abnâ' ad-dunyâ*, who had provided the pre-Islamic Persian Sasanian Empire with the same monied exploitive functionaries and cultured scribes, now largely Shi'ite but who still represented an eclectic mix of religious backgrounds and influences, including Nestorian Christian, Jewish, Zoroastrian and, by the end of the 4th/10th century, quasi-Buddhist. It was in this atmosphere especially, and among its sympathizers in Baghdad and elsewhere, that support for speculative thought and experimental research was cultivated, particularly in science, philosophy, alchemy, medicine, and literary anthologizing and criticism. Traditionalist Muslim piety and asceticism became interiorized and weakened in such centers.

Though Hallaj was recognized and indulged as a popular itinerant preacher (*wâ'iz*) with a mission, his language continued to become more abstract and dialectical in the mode of these non-traditionalist (Mu'tazilite and Shi'ite) proponents of philosophy (*falsafa*) in the patronized circles of the region.

Around 274/887, in his 30th year, he was arrested by Sunnite government agents and publicly whipped in Nahiyat al-Jabal, between Sus in Iran and Wasit in Iraq, probably a victim of mistaken identity as a political agitator, an agent of the Qarmathians, that radical left wing Shi'ite group bent explicitly on the overthrow of the 'Abbasid government and its supporters whom the latter suspected everyone critical of themselves to secretly be. There was a possibility, though no proof, of some moderate Shi'ite complicity sus-

The Facts of His Life and Theme of Disappearance 11

pecting him to be claiming the role of the *Mahdî*, whom he had preached was Jesus, who in his return would proclaim the final spiritual truth of truths and canonical path of paths. In fact, this incident may have marked his first publicly proclaimed identification with Jesus, though by no means implied conversion to Christianity, either then or at the times of his subsequent imprisonments and martyrdom when he would again cite and even call upon Jesus as an intercessor through the compassion of his shared suffering or when (in *Dîwân,* M.LVI, 1.2) he expresses his expectation of dying on the Cross and states that he no longer wishes to go to Mecca or Medina. Hallaj, in this same poem (1.1), is drawing on Qur'an 18 and the figure of the mystical guide of Sufis, al-Khadir, in his allusion to the "broken boat", and not implying that his concept of a spiritual journey and personal witness is based on rejection by Islam or of Islam, nor that his notion of "the disappearance of the self in God" belonged to any other realm than that of transcendence, not to culture, sociology, politics or membership in any other religion. His enemies questioned his sincerity, then and later, in vain, for his practise of Muslim piety remained strong in him always to the very end. They turned gradually instead to the possibility of mental imbalance, given some of his antics employed in gathering crowds in the market places to hear him preach; but this too gave way eventually to accusations of heresy. In fact, there was only one realm where the implications of his preaching of the period and afterwards could and did prove dangerous, the political, in which he himself no longer actively participated, after the Zanj revolt was quelled. But, then, religion and politics were separable only in the most ascetical of mystics' minds in the Community of Islam.

Throughout the five years that followed he traveled on his "mission" through the Arabicized centers of western Iran and Khurasan as far as the Oxus River, returning to his birthplace in Fars province where he settled for a time to write. In 280/893 he joined his wife in Ahwaz, where his third son Hamd was born toward the end of that year. It was there that he received the appellation *al-Hallâj al-asrâr* or *al-qulûb*, the carder or reader of the inner secrets of hearts, and where tales began to circulate regarding his performing of miracles, for which he stirred up accusations of charlatanism from both Muʿtazilites and Shiʿites, all of which gained him much notoriety and a wider following.

The traditional Sufi virtue of prudence was no more achievable by Hallaj than had been that of patience; and it is possible to imagine his character, albeit not stated literally as such, as drawn in this period of public celebrity even as his interior

The Facts of His Life and Theme of Disappearance 13

life deepened to a steadily profounder sense of private communion with God. This apparent contradiction or at least unsettling juxta-position was a source of anguish reflected on many levels in his poetry, especially when confusion had removed his center:

"I have tried to be patient, but how can my heart be patient when its center is gone?

Your Spirit mixed with my Spirit little by little, by turns, through reunions and abandons.

And now I am Yourself, Your existence is my own, and it is also my will.

You have ruled my heart, and I have wandered into every wadi.

My heart is closed, I have lost all sleep,

I am exiled, alone; how long will my solitude last?" (*Dîwân* M. XV and XVI)

The risk of connecting his poetry with his biography is great, of course, since he seldom if ever refers in his surviving works to events in his life, except for his anticipated martyrdom. Further, since most of his writings, along with those of his followers, were burned after his death, and those that survived did so in later histories or in the *dîwâns* of others or in carefully preserved eyewitness accounts and were not correctly reascribed for decades and, in some cases, not until our own time, the risk is multiplied. Nevertheless, the citation of his most experiential, personal poetry to illustrate his range of inner states, rather than outer events, seems appropriate and beneficial to the composition of an inner portrait. In all of his poetry "the center" is God and the experience realized in his words is the perilous embrace of God, which he makes clear transcends history and himself and in which his self at any moment and ultimately disappears. This therefore makes any suggested chronology secondary to his portrait.

Still, in 281/894 he made his second pilgrimage to Mecca via Basra and the Persian Gulf centers of Qarmathianism. He arrived at the Holy City, it was said, with four hundred disciples all dressed in rags and patches of the voluntary poor. He was accused this time by local Sufis of being possessed by jinn.

The following year he returned to Ahwaz and, after a brief stay in Tustar, he left the region for good with his wife and family and disciples, settling them in the already established Tustari textile quarter of Baghdad. He remained for a year in the capital city, during which he resumed contact with Sufis, especially with the more individualistic Nûrî (d. 295/907) and Shiblî (d. 334/945), the latter a Turk who had been a deputy of Caliph Muwaffaq and who retained connections with the powerful, but who would become a disciple and friend. He thereafter traveled by sea to India accompanied by an envoy of the then Caliph Mu'tadid.

The Facts of His Life and Theme of Disappearance

This marked the beginning of his second long 5-year journey in which his "mission" was intended to preach to Turkish infidels beyond the Oxus and to populations of western India who had been barely converted to Islam by radical Shi'ite missionaries. It was during this period that he made contact with notables of the ruling Samanid dynasty of Khurasan who would remain loyal to him against their allied and fellow-Sunnite 'Abbasid overlords of Baghdad at the time of his martyrdom in 309/922. He preached against Manichean dualism (*zandaqa*) among the Uyghur Turks and others beyond the *Dâr al-Islâm*, a heresy of which he himself would erroneously be accused at his trial. The spiritual balance in the world divided between forces of good and forces of evil could be struck, he preached, by means of self-sacrificing saints, the *abdâl* inter-cessors, who witness at the frontiers of true belief (*ahl al-thughûr wa'l-ribâtât*) so as to manifest love of God alone against temptations of evil.

His emphasis was focussed on the cultivation of the spiritual state of love (*mahabba*) leading through desire to union with God's essence (*'ishq dhâtî*), extending the teaching of such earlier mystics as Râbi'a and Muhâsibî as well as the elder Nûrî, to mention only a few.

Following his return to Baghdad, ca. 290-1/902-3, the emergence of opposition became more critical, reaching a higher level of seriousness in the person of a leading Zahirite expert in canon law and a sophisticated neo-Plationist writer on the subject of love, M. Ibn Dâwûd (d. 296/908), who initiated a legal denuciation against him (his *Fatwâ bi takfîr al-Hallâj*), which was proposed to Caliph Mu'tadid himself. It was thwarted by another distinguished canonist, the Shafi'ite Ibn Surayj (d. 305/917), who issued a disclaimer (*Fatwâ bi tawaqquf...hâl al-Hallâj*) stating that mystical inspiration (*ilhâm*), the long-standing issue associated with Hallaj and other of the so-called "ecstatic love mystics" in the minds of experts on the allowable and forbidden in religious law, was beyond the competence and jurisdiction of canon law.

Thus spared an official inquest, Hallaj undertook his third pilgrimage to Mecca, this lasting for two years of pious retreat, with continued meditation on the Qur'an, strict worship, purification of heart, leading, in his case, to reception of the gift of ecstatic speech (*shath*) in which the mystic pilgrim, stripped to the truth of his barest self, becomes the instrument of God's uttered word.

This is the final preparation of "the present witness" (*shâhid ânî*) of eternal love, which Hallaj's disciples believed him to be as confirmed by the sign of his extreme and prolonged piety and observance of the fundamental rituals of his Muslim faith. Included in his testimony was his expression, at 'Arafat, of his readiness to become

The Facts of His Life and Theme of Disappearance 17

a powerless victim, to suffer condemnation and death like Jesus, for the purification of his Community. He even beseeched God to let him die accursed by and for his brutalized, divided and decadent Islamic Community, even to become *kâfir*, an infidel, in order to be put to death, if necessary, "in the confession of the Cross," to arouse and unite all its members against him, and to effectively "disappear" in every aspect of himself through "Your love."

He left the holy cities of Mecca and Medina for the last time, returning to Baghdad via Jerusalem, which he reached on Holy Saturday 293/905. Resuming his life among his family, friends and followers in the Tustari quarter of the capital, he built a miniature Ka'ba, in which he celebrated symbolically and in private the *ta'rîf* and the ritual feasts of the Meccan pilgrimage. For this symbolic representation and his pronouncement that it was permitted to substitute it for the pilgrimage itself if one was unable for financial or health reasons to visit the Holy City according to the legal prescription, he was accused by his enemies then and at his eventual trial of preaching the overthrow of Islamic law. And this, despite the fact that there had been several historic precedents for such substitution, even by a caliph who had built a symbolic Ka'ba for his Turkish mercenaries at Samarra in the 830s. Also, in this period

Hallaj's preaching became more vehement and focussed precisely on his desire for martyrdom: in the name of the Sacred Law of Islam and for the common good.

He stirred again the opposition between canonists Ibn Dâwûd and Ibn Surayj over his case, as well as the support of a number of disciples in Samanid Khurasan and in Baghdad, including vizirs and other leaders of state and the young new Caliph Muqtadir's mother, the Greek Shaghab, a devoted disciple. Many of the latter saw in him an inspired and awaited leader called to reform the Community and its leaders to recognize and practise its revealed tenets of faith and personal and social values prescribed in the Qur'an. A remarkably large cross-section of notables and ordinary people looked to him for spiritual guidance, which placed him further in jeopardy as a threat to the then established political order and entrenched network of self-interests, especially illicit banking and speculation interests, operating counter to Islamic teaching throughout the empire. The Hallaj of this period had been foreseen in the Hallaj of the era of the Zanj revolt, only the conditions of corruption, greed, and oppression of the weak by those in power had greatly worsened and the Caliphate itself had fallen prey to unscrupulous bureaucrats, gold, silver and wheat speculators, and cruel taxfarmers, both

The Facts of His Life and Theme of Disappearance

Sunnite and Shi'ite in affiliation. Hallaj, it was hoped by such people, recognizing his popularity in Iraq and abroad, would confine himself to liturgical duties of the Community (prayer, pilgrimage, holy war of self-purification and conversion of infidels) and leave alone the malfeasance of profiteering public officials entrusted with the gathering of taxes and management of the Community treasury. His failure to withdraw and keep silent on the latter created a threat to public law and order, meaning to the continued drainage of the public trust into the pockets of officials on the hierarchical scale of manipulated power and exploitation.

On the support side, there was an extreme traditionalist Hanbalite Sunnite movement formed ca. 296/908 with expectation of removing the infant Muqtadir and his corrupt entourage of court advisers and replacing him with a rival caliph, Ibn al-Mu'tazz, and with Hallaj as the spiritual adviser of its chief architect, the Hanbalite Ibn Hamdân. The insurgency failed and Hallaj's fate, though seemingly buoyed further by the recurringly powerful traditionalists, was left decidedly vulnerable to the stronger prevailing currents of power politics; and Muqtadir's vizir, a Shi'ite, Ibn al-Furât, put him under surveillance.

Hallaj himself had not agreed to lead a movement aimed at temporal success, returning unofficially to a Sufi position in which a *fatâ*, a brother, renounces entirely any such desired end. Within a year, following subsequent aborted efforts by the Hanbalites, Hallaj's leading disciples were rounded up by the Baghdad police and he went into hiding in his homeland, again in Ahwaz, and later in Sus, a Hanbalite center. In 301/913 Hallaj's primary antagonist, Abû Muhammad Hâmid ibn al-'Abbâs (d. 311/923), the tax-farmer of Wasit and a palace banker of Caliph Muqtadir, took his place on the stage of the rising drama. Though a Sunnite trusted by the Sunnite Caliph, he had close family ties with militant Shi'ites who despised Hallaj for his assumption, in their minds, of the exclusive role of their awaited *Mahdî;* and as the paymaster of a Baghdad military garrison, he was in a powerful position to hunt down the charlatan, social agitator, heretic, overthrower of the Sacred Law, possessed by demons, and it was only a matter of time before his police and allies captured him and led him into Baghdad under close guard.

A rival force, also close to the weak Caliph Muqtadir, led by his mother, Shaghab, and a new vizir, 'Alî ibn 'Isâ, and one of the State secretaries, Hamd Qunnâ'î, all declared disciples of Hallaj, were able to prevent his case from going to a full trial, based on the earlier *fatwâ* of Ibn Surayj concerning the limits of the Law's jurisdiction in matters of mystical inspiration. Several of his disciples were released. Hallaj himself was given 3-days public exposure in the pillory with a placard around his neck calling him an "agent of the Qarmathians. " Hâmid was thus thwarted for the time being.

For the next 9 years, 301-308-9/913-921-2, Hallaj was confined in the palace, in effect under protective custody, by the Grand Chamberlain Nasr and other supporters, during which time his last works were written. Principal among these works was his prose *Tâ' Sîn al-Azal,* in which the Devil, Iblîs, is presented justifying himself as a pure monotheist, affirming God's transcendence by refusing to bow down before His unclean lowly creature man. This Iblîs is thus a higher mystic lover who witnesses the inaccessibility of God, but who through his extreme intellectualization of God as Pure Idea is unable to attain that humility necessary to accept the reality of His creativeness. Iblîs, in Hallaj's subtle monologue, marks the spiritual boundary of the mystic's hubris and dares to cross it through his defiant need of self-justification in order to attain his full tragic self-perception. It is an essay, as it were, in the form of fiction, and one profound in its insight into mysticism and the vagaries of self, and as disturbing as a reading of religious experience in its culture as St. John of the Cross's *Dark Night of the*

Soul and Dostoevsky's *Grand Inquisitor* are in theirs. Each reveals its author as a religious psychologist deeper than any found in our specialized fields of mysticism or psychology. Iblîs, in his way, as a Shi'ite neo-gnostic manichean, is a negative witness of the Unity of the One he professes only to love, and to love more purely, more uncompromisingly than humanity can. To Hallaj he is therefore a teacher of contemplative love, albeit a tragic figure of fatal self-deception. He is not a grotesque and ugly monster as in Dante's more materialistic depiction, nor a brief defiant tragic hero and ironic witness for liberty as in Milton's *Paradise Lost*, nor the ever manipulative and companionable deceiver of the ageing life-seeking academic Faust of Goethe's complex romance. Hallaj's Satan is an utterly solitary figure who can bear no companion but God, who aspires to no human quality given by God, whose message infused subconsciously, as it were, to humans is to believe that they themselves, because of their lower natures, can never attain God's Presence let alone be one with Him, that their true position is one of separation from God and despairing solitude (*infirâd*), a most fearful state that Hallaj wrote often of experientially in his poems of separation and solitude that followed moments of ecstatic union with his Beloved, those *awqât* that confirmed him in his disbelief in the satanic teaching that must have assaulted him during his long imprisonment. As a work, the *Tawâsîn* combines the major themes of his mission with the realized and centering experience of his life, in a dramatic form complementary to his lyric and didactic poetry.

Toward the end of his protective custody and due to a series of political vicissitudes that briefly brought the Shi'ite Ibn al-Furât back into vizirial power only to be replaced again by the Hallajian Ibn 'Isâ but this time in association with the main antagonist, Hâmid, Grand Chamberlain Nasr built Hallaj a private cell within the palace in which he could receive visitors but in which he was also more effectively confined. In 308/921 he was transferred "for about a year" to a prison, in which, according to his son Hamd's account, a separate building was erected where he could continue to receive visitors and from which he was able to pass through an adjoining door to read to and enjoin other prisoners to renew their faith in God.

When Ibn 'Isâ and Hâmid finally split over the former's inventory of the empire's budgetary resources, which Hâmid had been unlawfully draining off for his private use, the former tax-farmer tightened his alliance with Shi'ite bankers to engage the increasingly effete and money-needing Caliph in an illegal speculation on stocks of monopolized corn. Ibn 'Isâ and Nasr were able to rally the populist Hanbalites and tradesmen against the wholesalers and a riot ensued that was largely aimed against the 'Abbasid Caliphate for failing to uphold the fiscal and religious laws of Islam, a traditionalist as well as radical Shi'ite outcry raised on many occasions throughout Muslim history against presumptive leadership to a position (Caliph) always subject to questions of legitimacy. Hâmid was removed from power, but only temporarily. The forces of opposition to critics of unlawfully exercised power and those of potential popular riot were merely regrouping for the next occasion.

The next step in the progression toward the inevitable trial of Hallaj brought together, on the political plane, old enemies become allies through a common goal. The Greek eunuch Commander-in-chief, Mu'nis Qushûrî (d. 321/933), once closely allied to the Queen Mother Shaghab as head of the court harem, and to Grand Chamberlain Nasr, also of Greek origin, who had elevated him to Commander of field police forces, destined to lead the forces of the Caliphate of Muqtadir against the enemies of the Samanids, its allies, and later against the Daylamites in eastern Iran, returned to Baghdad, and this time came under the influence of Hâmid, whose intrigue was now aimed mostly against a prominent Samanid vizir, Bal'amî, the learned translator and patron of

The Facts of His Life and Theme of Disappearance

works transmitted in the "new Persian" language, and a disciple of Hallaj from earlier days. Despite the 'Abbasid-Samanid alliance and their common Sunnite tradition, it is tempting to compound the intensity of Hâmid's intriguing, beyond simple greed, with the recurring Middle Eastern subtext of Arab versus Persian ethnocentricity, particularly in light of the fact that the 4th/10th century would see the political and cultural eclipse of the 'Abbasid Caliphate and its patronage of virtually all but the Arabic religious sciences by the ascension of Persian dynasties and the dynamic flowering of New Persian literature. But such historic consciousness and foreboding may be too much to ascribe to this brutal tax-farmer from the near-legendary Umayyad governor Hajjâj's town of Wasit.

In order to regain power with the fickle and always manipulatable Caliph Muqtadir, Hâmid, with Mu'nis's support, set a plot to ruin the Caliph's most trusted officials, Ibn 'Isâ and Nasr, as being too soft in fiscal policy vis-à-vis the general populace and thus weakening the treasury for flexible (i.e., usurious) investment of resources and consequently diminishing the Caliph's support for self-indulgences. Hâmid posed, as before, as a defender of a hard fiscal policy. This time Hallaj became the clear instrument for his return to power by being a favorite of Ibn 'Isâ and Nasr and by his "heresy", if brought to trial, would reflect directly on them. The plot was set in motion by Hâmid's persuading Muqtadir, over his mother's protests, to remove Vizir Ibn 'Isâ from Hallaj's case to be brought customarily before the Vizirial Court, and Nasr from custody of his person in his confinement. A further figure, Ibn Mujâhid, the leader of the body of Qur'an reciters and an enemy of Hallaj and other such mystics, approved the process. Hallaj's Hanbalite traditionalist supporters staged a demonstration on his behalf against Hâmid on the same grounds as before, a demonstration led by one of Hallaj's most faithful disciples, one of the official *shuhûd*, the upright witnesses, at his trial, Ibn 'Atâ'. But the demonstration only served the plot by showing that Hallaj and his followers were a threat to law and order. The elder distinguished historian and Sunnite moderate Tabarî (d.310/923), though a friend of Ibn 'Isâ, refrained from involvement in the case on grounds of his rejection of violence, which led the Hanbalites to demonstrate in turn outside his house.

In late March 922 (Qa'da 309) Hâmid, in full ascendancy as vizir, with his Hallajian rivals removed from positions of power through his brutal maneuvering, and with the Cahiph's mandate to guarantee public order by any means, pushed the trial, judgement, and execution to conclusion.

The Facts of His Life and Theme of Disappearance 27

Easily compliant judges and legal experts who had earlier facilitated the smear of lawless Qarmathianism against Hallaj now fixed on his substitution of a private pilgrimage for the legal obligation owed to Mecca as the prime evidence of his seeking to overthrow the Sacred Law of Islam. Hâmid had Ibn 'Ata', one of Hallaj's closest disciples and also a legal expert who refused to sign the declaration of his guilt, murdered before the end of the trial; some sources have him committing the act himself. Last minute efforts by the Grand Chamberlain Nasr and the Queen Mother Shaghab to persuade Caliph Muqtadir to reverse the vizirial court's decision led to a brief countermanding of the execution, which eventually he approved, however, under Hâmid's prodding, along with the most extreme form of punishment sought by the vizir.

Hamd's account (*Akhbâr,* no. 2) presents his father as completing his pre-dawn ritual prayer, and then repeating over and over the word *makr,* "illusion", until night almost ended. Then, after a long silence, he cried out the word *al-Haqq,* "The Truth". Then he wrapped himself in his cloak, turned in the direction of Mecca, and spoke his *munâjât,* ecstatic prayers.

We are here, we, Your witnesses.
We are seeking refuge in the splendor of Your glory

In order that You reveal Yourself as You desire,
O You who are God in heaven and God on earth.
It is You who shine forth when You desire
Just as You shone forth Your divine decree
In the most beautiful form in Adam,
The form in which the enunciating spirit resides
Present in knowledge and in speech, in will and in existence.
How is it that You who were present in my self
After they had stripped me of my self
Who used my self to proclaim Your self
Revealing the truth of my knowledge and my miracles
Drawn from my ascensions to the Thrones
Of Your pre-eternities to utter the Word which creates me,
Now wish me to be seized, imprisoned, judged,
Executed, hung on the gibbet, my ashes to be thrown
To the sandstorms that will scatter them
And the waves of the Tigris that will play with them...
I weep to You for the souls whose present witness
Goes now beyond the Where to meet the witness of eternity.
I cry to You for hearts so long refreshed

By clouds of revelation, which once filled up
with seas of wisdom.
I cry to You for the Word of God, which since
it perished
Has faded into nothing in our memory.
I cry to You for signs that have been gathered
up by intellects,
Now nothing reminds of them except debris.
I cry to You, I swear it by Your love,
For the witness of those whose only mount for
reaching You was silence.
All have crossed the desert, leaving neither
well nor trace behind,
Vanished like the 'Ad tribe and their lost city
of Iram.
And after them the abandoned crowd is
muddled on their trails,
Blinder than beasts, blinder even than she-
camels.

The narrative of Hamd, after presenting the two prayers, proceeds to the execution as follows: Then he was quiet.

After that, his faithful servant, Ibrâhîm ibn Fâtik, said to him: "Master, bequeath me a maxim. My father replied: "One's fault-filled self (*'uyûb an-nafs*) must be overcome or it will overcome one."

When morning came, they led him from his prison, and I saw him walking jubilantly in his chains, reciting: "My companion, so as not to appear to wrong me, made me drink from his own cup, as a host treats a guest; but as soon as the cup had passed from hand to hand, He made the leather execution mat be brought and the sword; thus it falls to him who drinks wine with the lion in the height of summer."

They led him then to the esplanade where before an enormous crowd they cut off his hands and feet after having flogged him with 500 lashes of the whip.

In the account of 'Attâr (Arberry tr., *Tadhkirat*, 270-271) he is said to have "rubbed his bloody, amputated hands over his face, so that both his arms and his face were stained with blood."

"Why did you do that?" people enquired.

"Much blood has gone out of me," he replied. "I realize that my face will have grown pale. You suppose that my pallor is because I am afraid. I rubbed blood over my face so that I might appear rose-cheeked in your eyes. The cosmetic of heroes is their blood."

"Even if you bloodied your face, why did you stain your arms?"

"I was making ablution."

"What ablution?"

"When one prays two *rak'as* in love," Hallaj replied, "the ablution is not perfect unless performed in blood."

"The executioners then plucked out his eyes; he was then stoned by the crowd, after which they cut off his ears and nose. He uttered his forgiveness of them as they were preparing to cut out his tongue. An old woman shouted, "What right has this little wool carder (*hallâj*) to speak of God?" Thereafter, he uttered "It is enough for the lover to diminish himself before the uniqueness of the One." Then his tongue was cut out, and, finally, he was beheaded at the time of the evening prayer."

In Hamd's account, which corresponds in most details to that of Sulamî (d. 412/1021; *Ta'rîkh as-sûfîya*), after the flaggelation Hallaj was hoisted up onto the gibbet (*suliba*) and I heard him talking ecstatically with God: "O my God, here am I now in the dwelling place of my desire, where I contemplate Your marvels. O my God, since You witness friendship even to whoever does You wrong, how is it You do not witness it to this one to whom wrong is done because of You?"

Afterwards I saw Abû Bakr Shiblî, who approached the gibbet, cry out very loudly, the following verse: "Have we not forbidden you (the gibbet) to receive any guest, man or angel?

Then he asked him: "What is Sufism?" He answered: "The lowest degree one needs for attaining it is the one you behold." Shiblî asked further: "What is the highest degree?" Hallaj responded: "It is out of reach for you; but tomorrow you will see; for it is part of the divine mystery that I have seen it and that it remains hidden to you."

At the time of the evening prayer, the authorization by the Caliph to decapitate Hallaj came. But is was declared by the officer in charge: "It is too late: we shall put it off until tomorrow."

When morning came, they took him down from the gibbet and dragged him forth to behead him. I heard him cry out then, saying in a very high voice: 'All that matters for the ecstatic is that his Only One bring him to His Oneness."

Then he recited his verse: "Those who do not believe the Final Hour call for its coming; but those who believe in it await it with loving shyness knowing that this will be the coming of God." These were his last words.

His head was cut off, then his trunk was rolled up in a straw mat, doused with fuel, and burned.

Later, they carried his ashes to the minaret on the Ra's al-Manara promontory beside the Tigris to disperse them to the wind.

Hâmid and his associates hoped that the public display of Hallaj's head, first hung on the prison wall and afterwards carried throughout the Samanid districts of Khurasan, would dissuade would-be social reformers, religious purists, and wavering political allies from opposition to 'Abbasid Caliphal (i.e., vizirial) banking and speculation policies. Behind the cynical tax-farmer become vizir were many financial and religious figures whose interests were served by his aggressive policies. Notable among these was a crafty and,

The Facts of His Life and Theme of Disappearance

with respect to Hallaj, jealous Shi'ite mystic, Shalmaghânî, who manipulated the monomania of the old scoundrel into worsening the punishment of Hallaj as eternal damnation for sorcery (Q. 20:74; 5:33; 26:49) and who was himself put to death in 322/933 in the same manner as his rival. Hâmid was himself killed by a Baghdad mob in 311/924 after being paraded through the streets stuffed in a pig skin.

In summary, we can say that the world to Hallaj was in a serious condition caused by humans afflicted with moral compromise and blindness, the roots of which were self-indulgence, greed, officially condoned cruelty, decadence, all things separating the Community from God, true guidance, and grace. As with Hasan of Basra long before him, the darkness had to be recognized and offset by self-examination and ascetical purification rather than by mere criticism of others. But unlike the celebrated progenitor of Muslim mystical *ascèse*, Hallaj based his personal mission and witness of the transcendent source Himself, on the One he called Beloved or Friend or You and ultimately his Only Self. His concentration from the time of his first *hajj* to Mecca was on the overwhelming relationship with the Real, the One Creative Truth, *al-Haqq*, a relationship whose threshold was "spiritual anguish" (*Dîwân* M.XVII) and whose destiny, in his own case, was condemnation and death at the hands of jealous and manipulative government and religious bureaucrats. And after his death, for centuries, even to the present day, he has remained a subject of controversy and devotion, of denial and affection: on the one hand, examined by those traditionalist experts in Islamic Sacred Law and Shi'ite legitimists bent on preserving their respective notions of authority; and on the other hand, revered by disciples and ordinary folk preserving and transforming his name into legend. Later we shall touch on one highly influential traditionalist reexamination and support for the verdict, extreme punishment, and execution given Hallaj, that of Ibn Taymîya (d. 728/1328).

II

"So kill me now my faithful friends
for in my killing is my life."
-*Dîwân*, LM ed. Qasîda X; Sh. ed. 14.

THE RESURFACING OF HIS LIFE AND ITS REPEATED IMPACT

It is the death of Hallaj as told by eyewitnesses and kept alive in popular and literary accounts by later mystics, biographers and historians that transcends the remoteness of his time and brings him close to us. That he was warned when a very young apprentice Sufi by Junayd and others among his masters who were less headstrong and passionate than he that his death would be violent, public, and the result of a condemnation of dire legal and spiritual consequences became a crucial part of his legend. Fictional most probably, though like ingredients accruing to form a myth around a real heroic and historic figure, the inclusion of his long anticipation, acceptance, and finally welcoming of his death became his singular most unsettling attribute. This attribute should underscore for students of comparative mysticism that this old and highly sophisticated tradition of Sufism had in his time drawn its boundaries and thresholds not to cross, having pushed its way to those limits theoretically and experimentally, in its Khurasan and Baghdad schools, prior to him, especially on the forbidden incarnational matter of the experience of personal union with God. Other mystics such as Dhû'l-Nûn, Bâyezîd Bistâmî, Nûrî, Tirmidhî, and Ibn 'Atâ', to mention just a few cited previously who are also subjects of this series, had also meditated the possibility of this experience as their mystical goal and understood its risks. Hallaj was thus part of a tradition and, more particularly, of only one emphasis within that tradition that was older than himself and that would survive the horror of his death. Junayd and other advocates of the "sobriety" (*sahw*) versus the "intoxication" (*sukr*) emphasis seem to have understood the dangers to the tradition of separate, individual inspiration (*ilhâm*) as verified by the death of Hallaj. For their heirs and for most traditionalists over the centuries he also became a legend proving the wisdom of the forbidden. For both enthusiastic supporters and prudent rejectors of the way of a Hallaj the death itself was thus the doorway to myth. And Husayn ibn Mansûr "*al-Hallâj*" has this remarkable transhistoric power of myth to stir deep emotion and imagination in an entire culture and beyond.

The Resurfacing of His Life and its Repeated impact

For the folk so-called his mythic power and the legend of his life come in the form of consolations through retellings of his sufferings: consolations to victims of injustice or disease or mothers in the pains of childbirth or barren women yearning to give birth to a "saint of love" like Hallaj. That he knew he would die on the gibbet under the weight of Sacred Law that he upheld even as he cried out for help from his fellow Muslims to save him from God (*Akhbâr* 38; note Q. 72:22 = "no one can save me from God.") becomes the inspiration and impetus of repeated tellings of his story and callings upon him for intercession. In each retelling one is made to face its full reality and, in asking why it happened, one is made to see the convergence of historical forces and personages moving or, in a Tolstoian sense, moved by them; and beyond all that, one sees this rather small 64-year old man whose intimacy with his known yet unknowable God finds its desired fulfillment through this terrifying and officially sanctioned death. Hallaj arouses hostility and denial yet also gives consolation. His death is his personal seal on his beliefs and his authentication, not to be imitated or seen as the highest rung on the mystical ladder, as he told his friend Shiblî, but the proof of his unwavering devotion — and not merely to a principle, but to the One he knew as his Self who made him forget his own name through his complete immersion (*istighrâq*) in love. The lived text of his life and death reveals the teachings he absorbed from the Qur'an, first and foremost, and secondarily from other influences, Christian, Hellenistic, neo-Gnostic, current in his time. Discussion among scholars concerning his "orthodoxy", pro and con, and his efforts at synthesis found in his more didactic and philosophical writings continues to the present-day (note the discussion Massignon reviews at length in *Passion,* 2nd ed., Eng. tr. v.1, p.518 ff: "The Hallajian *Testament of Faith*"). But beyond this indeed serious question remains the dogmatic intensity of his practiced faith and the sweetness of his intimacy of love for God and for humanity expressed in his lyric poetry. Apart from the legality or political exigency of his appalling execution and the questions that persist regarding either, one receives ripples of fright at the thought that faith could lead one to such an end in any civilized society. And Islamic society was indeed civilized in Hallaj's time, with all the accoutrements of culture, manners, learning and sophistication current in its cities, especially Baghdad. Indeed the wealth and patronage for humane learning and scientific research in a variety of areas, including literature, law, mathematics, medicine, astronomy, and traditional religious sciences, was at one of its apogees in Islam. The form, indeed the fact, of such an execution was thus and still remains an unresolved shock to the civilization through those aware of it. One reaction current today among many retraditionalists romanticizing the heights and omitting the contradictions is to deny it ever happened or to claim by interpolation of "facts" into old sources that it may have happened but to someone else of no importance, not to someone of this man's following and obvious importance: an interpolation process common enough in Hallaj's own time and recurring often enough in ours. Meanwhile a man known by many as "al-Hallâj" continues to dance in his chains on the esplanade of historic memory. He remains *there,* in that place. People touch him as he passes through them, some to strike him, to push him further away, some to grasp at his clothing or his beard for a possible relic, mesmerized by the publicity of his coming death, and some to reassure and even make known their presence as a consolation. No shallow sentiment involved, no false sincerity, no claim to prophethood, sainthood or messiahhood, in this "witness" who dared to speak of God as "You. Between lovers who can say who is the lover, who the beloved?" The sober rememberer of this day or of any others it brings to mind in other civilizations at their self-proclaimed apogees needs relief from memory, a pause that is prolonged, not allowing serious reflection but only a return to one's own everyday life of incidentals and absurdities, in which even traces of yearning for God must not persist and keep one in a state of at least semi-anxiety: a state in which the so-called Hallajian way takes root and Hallaj resurfaces with his direct transparent expressions of love and he is once again on that esplanade and we are in the mob, even as supposedly detached historians, uncertain as to what our arms and minds are reaching for or against. To resolve our uncomfortable dilemma we look to the authorities that issued the condemnation, and laugh a little in relief from the terror that it could ever happen to oneself. One is protected at last from oneself by authority, serving in the Community of Islam's name, that puts such a heretic and public enemy to death. Only God the Merciful the Compassionate truly knows and provides.

"Did you not know," one anguished Sufi shouted at the gibbet, "you were not to receive a guest?" and threw a rose at the guest's heart, at the bleeding Husayn ibn Mansûr who read hearts.

We are hosts as humans to our guests, we are not gibbets. It cannot be God who does this thing, the most troubled Sufis argue inwardly and among themselves; not the Essence of Hospitality, the Essence of all Desire. But it cannot be other than God also, for it is God's Law that has decreed the punishment for heresy, for likening oneself to God.

A vivid recollection of Hallaj's martyrdom brings spiritual and human contradiction. For most, as we mentioned before, denial is the only recourse. God couldn't permit the execution in His Law's name of an innocent; therefore, this Hallaj was given the punishment to preserve the truth of God's teaching and Law. Justice was done. Or, from another perspective, how could Hallaj have loved his ultimate Judge and punisher? Only if he rose above himself in some way to celebrate his own annihilation, his *fana'*. Thus we can feel more reassured in our pain at his suffering and can deny our fear and sorrow, even as we turn to accept the trial God gives us for our sakes. Our self is our source of agony, as Hasan of Basra said and as Hallaj restated when he said to a disciple: "Master your self lest your self master you." He recognized the evil in himself and welcomed God's annihilation of his self. The path of extreme asceticism leading to mystical love is truly dangerous, for it teaches annihilation of self; it leads one to painful punishment, to the death of Hallaj.

The law of moderation, of devout obedience, not intoxication and ecstasy and experience of God Himself outside the prescriptions of the Law, is the only proper path of life for one, for us, for all those who would transcend suffering brought on by self. It is the majority's way of denying a "witness" like Hallaj a place in the heart or even access to "reading" and stirring one's desires. The only sure guidance is God's as given in His "reading". The rest is self and its presumptions. We can accept Hallaj's poetry as edifying and pure to a point. But his death was ordained, accepted by him, and enacted as a protection for us not as a way for us to follow. Still, he is dancing in his chains. He is hanging on the gibbet. His image surfaces.

Louis Massignon (1883-1962), in his magisterial study of Hallaj, saw this mystic's martyrdom as central to the spiritual development of Islamic history, whereas many scholars, Western and Islamic, have viewed it as marginal and anomalous to it; and, while admiring the noted French scholar's erudition and his remarkable belief, as a Catholic, in the authenticity of the Qur'anic inspiration as coming from the God of Abraham and in his steadfastness in support of this contention, some have scored him for exaggerating the importance of such an obscure and largely forgotten figure or indeed of any individual "hero" of any time and any place. Yet, leaving the case of Massignon and his critics and admirers aside, as he himself would've wished in deference to the teaching and, in his view, the "witness" of Hallaj himself, this obscure figure resurfaces across time and causes repeatedly the same hatred and veneration in political and religious circumstances when drawn together into crucibles of suffering as if to test in the absence of human justice the Justice of God. Hallaj is by his teaching and his death a historic archetype within and beyond his civilization, regardless of the degree of importance his actual person may have had. He resurfaces as an archetype for simple people seeking intercessory hope, as mentioned before, and for notable poets and dramatists, such as Adonis, Bayati and Sabbûr in the modern secular Arab world, whose sense of social injustice and whose compassion and integrity of belief find correspondence and hope in this obscure and almost forgotten Hallaj.

While he may not represent, as Massignon argued, an "axial point' in the religious culture of Islam, he evokes many of its historic contradictions and was subject to many of its principal recurring themes. A review of such is not inappropriate for our understanding of this mystic and his fate.

Though it is surely an exaggeration to suggest that Hallaj was fully aware of his historic importance or of his role as a magnet attracting the major themes of his civilization to himself, he did find himself conflicted by a series of dichotomies, two of which were admirably reflected by the 14th century social historian Ibn Khaldûn (d. 808/

1406): the theme of the sedentary versus the nomadic with its roots in the ancient Near Eastern depictions of declining citadel civilizations and emerging tribal peoples from the Steppe; and the theme of *asabiyya* or group-tribal solidarity as the binding social and even religious force in the early Arab configurations. It is not too fanciful to suggest that the fourth/tenth century recurrences or variations on these themes affecting Hallaj were the dichotomies and apparent contradictions between institutional and individual religious vocations, between literal adherence to the text of Revealed Law and the emergence of serious testimonies of direct experience, that had become intensified since the aforementioned Hasan of Basra and Râbi'a al-'Adawîya with the development of mystical schools and systematic manuals demonstrating and guiding "states and stages" of experience and arguing the boundaries of Sacred Law vis-à-vis the temptations and impulses of such experience. Secondly, Hallaj and many other mystics like himself of Persian origin, sons or grandsons of converts from Zoroastrianism or Greek Christianity, found themselves caught in the ethnic tension between Persian and Arab cultures with Arabic being the dominant "institutional" culture drawn from the Qur'anic Sacred Law and Arab scholars being the primary "world-builders" of Islamic tradition. Further, as mysticism itself became more systematized and "institutionalized" into "schools", more boundaried, more "civilized", the impulses of direct mystical experience became still more radicalized. The civilized prudence of a Junayd, the head of the Baghdad school of Sufis, signified the development of an '*asabiyya* not unlike that found earlier in each of the "orthodox" Sunnite schools of law, each *madhhab*, at least its foreshadowing, that would be realized fully in Sufism with the establishment of brotherhoods, the *futuwwa* orders, in the seventh/thirteenth century. Louis Massignon (Abr.*Passion*, p. 102) wrote the following regarding Hallaj's break with official Sufism:

"Hallaj broke away, because he was worn out by spiritual dryness and the hypocritical "fraternal corrections" of those hermits who cultivate their perfection sealed off from reality, keeping for them-selves the words of life that could save others and only intoxicate themselves."

Though the comment is more insightful than literal, it underscores the historical fact of a professional structuring that led Hallaj and other individualistic mystics mentioned previously as being like him to forego the support and security of a movement, a school, a group consciousness, without however denouncing the tradition of Sufism or its religion of Islam; indeed they conceived their actions as spontaneous and vital renewals of both and were revered as such by later mystics who reabsorbed them institutionally, such as 'Attâr (d. 626/1229) and Rûmî (d. 672/1273).

As for the matter of ethnic tension, those Persians writing in Arabic like Hallaj, who did not know the Persian of his time and who preceded the later fourth/tenth century development of New Persian and the beginnings of its great literary renascence that would over-shadow Arabic in both profane and mystical poetry, were obliged to focus almost exclusively by necessity on issues of Arabic Muslim Law and traditionalism and within their didactic literary frameworks offered only moments of spontaneous lyric mystical flights. Within both the fields of law and of mysticism, which were by no means inherently exclusive of one another, a significant number of the leaders were of Persian origin and were personally sympathetic to Hallaj and other such mystics but were fearful of any variance from mainstream Arabicized institutional authority: especially in Sacred Law and in Caliphal politics whose only legitimate purpose was to uphold it.

A Hallaj appeared by consequence a radical individualist through his rejection of "spiritual dryness" and through the public display of his "conversations with God" (*shath*) and his calling upon the Justice of God (the *sayha bi'l-Haqq*) against the decadent wasteful unegalitarian political establishment in Baghdad. On the other hand, the radical Shi'ites, as mentioned before, who were internal opponents of the Sunnite establishment's basis of authority, found a Hallaj appearing to assume their long-standing *extra*-religio-political basis of authority as defined by their quasi-mystical hidden *Imâm*, who in his awaited time, would usher in the era of Divine Justice. The '*asabiyya* theme and force in society had long since assumed a sectarian coloration and as such had the power, from their different perspectives, to polarize individual "witnesses" against the Community and to isolate their testimonies as "heretical".

A further variation on the '*asabiyya* theme, to be touched on only briefly here with regard to Hallaj, was the neo-Hellenistic movement which found its impetus and at least partial legitimacy with the patronage under Caliph al-Ma'mûn of the *Bayt al-hikma* translation center in the early decades of the third/ninth century. The center injected a new rival tradition into the Islamic Community and with it a new critical approach to traditionalist learning and knowledge. The Qur'an (18:19) states most suggestively, "We awakened them that they might question one another." Again, it is not fanciful to consider one correspondence between the Qur'anic *kahf* and Plato's legend of the cave at least symbolic of the conflict between the Qur'anic traditionalists and the new speculative dogmatists, the so-called Mu'tazilites, that would dominate the intellectual atmosphere for the rest of the century and establish permanently yet another quasi-sectarian dichotomy within Islam. Without reiterâting the many issues on which traditionalism and Mu'tazilism fixed their irreconcilable differences, the primary difference was surely the matter of "questioning" itself: the subjects permitted to be open to questioning, and the freedom of the individual to question. Questioning existed in both of these "traditions", but the contemporary emergence of movements of "retraditionalization" remind us of the attitudes and tensions dominating the atmosphere of Hallaj's time in which commentaries on the Qur'anic questioning cited above were aimed at strengthening ritual observance and a deeper understanding of obedience to God, against the laxity in observance and morals of the new philosophical questioners and speculators and the Community's cultural elite who had patronized them at least privately when traditionalists regained the political upperhand. For Hallaj the language of philosophical inquiry affected permanently the pedagogy of orthodox mysticism and the analysis of its first-hand experience; like the Thomist St. John of the Cross, the lexically neo-Hellenistic Hallaj both analyzed systematically and lived his mystical experience. He was not unique among Sufis in this, nor given the atmosphere could he have been otherwise. Mysticism was a formal, structured, ritualized discipline, and could only be extended to actualized union through more, not less, of the same. But Hallaj was from all accounts a traditionalist whose "mission" was to reanimate ritual observance and share through public preaching and spontaneous evocation his deeper understanding of obedience to God. But, again, he found himself in the midst of what were apparent contradictions to others. It should not come as a surprise that among Hallaj's strongest supporters and key instigators of public demonstrations on his behalf at the end were arch traditionalists, the Hanbalites and Hanbalite educated, and his principal enemies were political and religious bureaucrats and aesthetes who found their interests best served by the corrupt Caliphal and Vizirial establishment.

Much of Hallaj's fate lay with a very basic recurring theme in Islam, one indeed underlying all of the aforementioned themes and apparent contradictions; namely, the problem of authority whose resolutions generated conflict and disunity. The assumption, based on Qur'anic revelation, among the true believers of Islam, is that authority, throughout time, is vested only in God, not in any mortal being or idol claimed by mortals to represent God. Authority is thus a transcendent principle and an attribute reserved to God alone. The authority of the Prophet, and that of his immediate four so-called Rightly Guided Successors, on a secondary plane to his, is owed entirely to God and, according to the majority of Muslims, has not been continued historically since. Authenticity of experience, spiritual or secular, as a consequence could only be attained by extreme self-sublimation and humility before God, achievable only by practise of the ritual duties of the faith and strict adherence to the commandments of God as explicitly revealed in the Qur'an. Such authenticity is achieveable and sought by humans but does not invest them with divine authority. Hallaj's claim to union with God to the point where God was his "only Self" made him vulnerable to accusations of forbidden associationism, something the early Mu'tazilities believed by their enlightened questioning they were helping to eliminate from orthodox Islam. But as we know, in the end it was not the orthodox traditionalist Muslims targetted for such enlightenment nor mainstream Shi'ites *en groupe* who thought him a "heretic" worthy of death.

In the eighth/fourteenth century, however, a major Hanbalite traditionalist, Ibn Taymîya (728/1328), reexamined the trial and execution of Hallaj and concluded the condemnation and terms were just. Louis Massignon, in the 2nd volume of his *Passion of al-Hallaj* (Eng. ed., pp. 45-49), presents in full three of Ibn Taymîya's *fatwas*

The Facts of His Life and Theme of Disappearance

justifying the condemnation carried out four centuries earlier against the mystic, in an effort, Massignon believed, to condemn the one whom he considered ("mistakenly") "the forerunner... of the monism introduced by Ibn 'Arabî (d.638/1240). He therefore persecuted his memory with particular intensity, inflamed perhaps by the persistent devotion that some Hanbalites still had for this condemned man."

(1) The answer to two questions concerning Hallaj:

1st question: Is this an honest (*siddîq*) or perfidious (*zindîq*) man? Is this a venerable saint (*walî muttaqî*), the possessor of a divine grace (*hâl rahmânî*) or an adept at magic; and

2nd question: Was he executed for *zandaqa* in accordance with the opinion of the assembly of *'ulamâ'* of Islam? or was he in fact unjustly (executed)?

Answer: Hallaj was justly condemned. And anyone who is not of this opinion is either hypocritical or ignorant; and whoever approves of him must be killed like him.

After recounting his life and travels, some details of his writings' subjects, trials and punishments, Ibn Taymîya concludes he was an unrepentant satanic being.

(2) In another *fatwâ* he dismisses with equal ferocity any claim the followers may make to the sanctity of Hallaj based on his practices, his ecstasies and various utterances, and his ideas. He

concludes in speaking "for us '*ulamâ*', we have the formula of divine unity (*Tawhîd*) which has been prescribed for us, the way of God that has been laid down for us, and from both we have learned, that "what Hallaj said is only falsehood" (quoting Ibn Dâwûd, Hallaj's rival) and that those like him deserve death."

(3) In a third *fatwâ*, Ibn Taymîya reiterates many of Hallaj's own Sufi contemporaries' opinions opposing his extreme mysticism of union with God:

A. Ecstasy had temporarily cut off his reason, he spoke in amorous delirium;

B. He was lucid and he revealed the mystery, even that of *Tawhîd*, which made his execution necessary.

Hallaj, he concludes, was not pardonable based on excuses of (A), but was in fact lucid and was thus rightly condemned for blasphemy against the Qur'an and his teaching that the *hajj* could be performed fully outside Mecca. He was thus a sorcerer served by demons.

Traditionalism would seem to have thus resurfaced effectively by its very opposition to a resurfaced mystical deviation in a continuous dialectic through time. Apologetics continued its process of worldbuilding, albeit on a greatly reduced scale following the Mongol invasion of Baghdad in 1258 AD and with it the termination of the 'Abbasid Caliphate and its illusion of authority.

III

THE PROBLEM OF UNIVERSALISM

One of the likely causes for antipathy to Hallaj, both his person and his teaching, stems in part from his many travels through foreign lands and his association with persons of other faiths and beliefs. There is more than a little Arab ethnocentricity in the severity of Ibn Taymîya's reaffirmation of the condemnation and indeed in his post-Mongol ethnically dispersed and beleagured notion of "us 'ulamâ".' Hallaj was, as he believed inwardly Muhammad his Prophet to be, a universalist on all levels while remaining a practitioner of a particular ritual path, that of Islam.

On the level of Islam's relation with the other Abrahamic religions of the monotheistic revelation, he had this to say (Abr. *Passion,* p. 104; Vol. 1, pp. 193-4):

"I have pondered as to how to give religious
    faiths an experimental definition
And I formulate it as a single Principle with
    many branches.
Do not demand therefore that your compan-

> ion in discussion adopt this or that confessional denomination.
> That would prevent him from arriving at honest union (with you and with God).
> It is up to the Principle Himself to come to this man, and to clarify
> In him all of the supreme meanings: and then this man will understand (everything).

He was accused by his enemies of dissimulation and opportunism by associating with neo-Helenists, philosophers, aesthetes, pseudo-mystics, magicians, Christians, Jews, Zoroastrians, Manichaeans, Hindus, Buddhists, the rich and the poor, indiscriminately on his travels throughout the Near East, Iran, India and possibly even China; and at home with adepts of radical Shi'ism while claiming the heritage and identity of a strict traditionalist.

He represented in this regard a persistent recurrence in Islam of the impulse for universalism versus the fearful retrenchment and consolidation preached by so many of the ascetical and politically motivated traditionalists to the common people and literalists they influenced, if not controlled through their schools. His was the mentality of a traveler who found God as the Host of the worlds and hospitality thus as universal, not merely a cultural phenomenon among Arabs or

The Problem of Universalism

any other single ethnic group, while many others, both Shi'ite and Sunnite, Persian and Arab, believed God was their Qur'anic totem exclusive to themselves: the monotheistic sin, as it has been called by modern religious universalists. What kept Hallaj from syncretism was his steadfast undeniable practise of his faith, which did not seem to him a contradiction to his universalism: because his Beloved was the source of everything to him and was free in His creativeness, His compassion, and His hospitality.

(*Passion*, vol. 1,p. 194:) "Understand, my brothers — God grant to you and to us the good fortune of being in His grace — that observance (*'ibâda*) is the fruit of knowledge... Indeed, this is the road to joy, the route to Paradise...; obedience to God (*tâ'a*) is our indispensable provision...": meaning fulfillment of the Sacred Law's obligations.

For Hallaj, who believed in the Law of Unity, its divine Reality was not negated by the seemingly ubiquitous evidence of social and political and religious disunity in the this-worldly sense, but by the narrow supposed higher affirmation of God's Unity by the convinced pietists, and in the highest pietistic sense by the angelic witness, Iblîs, whom, Hallaj questioned unto self-revelation during his long imprisonment.

The Truth was universal to Hallaj; it was God Himself, the freer from self, the resolver of contradictions, the One whom he adored in His Unity and Singularity unto the disappearance of himself. The *Tawhîd* was the realization beyond the rungs of one's asceticism, ecstasies, and martyrdom, as uttered to Shiblî.

To Satan, the narrowest monotheist, who disregards all but Transcendent Unity, however, and considers the existence of humanity an aberration to be rejected, there is no Unity in which such contradiction is resolved to his purist satisfaction. Satan's only recourse in his intransigent state, is to teach human beings that they are separate from God, by dualizing being, and making himself "the third", "the only one who separates each of you — in order to proclaim You Holy. "(*Passion,* vol. 1, p. 483)

The mystic lovers, such as Hallaj and his forerunners (Nûrî) and followers (Ibn 'Atâ'), are therefore the dialoguers (wrestlers in the old Biblical sense) with the Devil, for they cross in their love the threshold of the forbidden by desiring the Judgement of God alone and accepting the Judgement carried out by man in receiving, even unto agony and death, the ecstasy of the one's illumination as the sanctification of their hearts. The difference between the accursed saint and the fallen angel, apart from the distinction in their natures, is in the one's surrendering of his heart to the sanctifying grace of the Uniting Spirit and in the other's self-deception of a scorned lover unable to bear the Divine Fire's action of extending to others His secret of eternal life.

"Desire is the fire from the Light of the primordial Fire... the fire of Desire inflames them with Reality whether they are near to it or far." (Hallaj, Abr. *Passion,* p. 173)

Evil comes thus not from some inherent brutishness in a prejudged base nature of man, despite the satanic view of such and the manifestations of brutishness in the world, but from the spiritually blinding jealousy caused by misdirected love that leads the embittered to accelerate the world's and his own self-destruction.

As indicated before, see *Passion,* vol. 3, pp. 306-327, for the text and full discussion of *Tâ Sîn' al-Azal.* Here follows further excerpts relevant to the present study and to the universalist theme.:

"My mind is going mad because of You !
What is Adam? Nothing but for You !
Who am I then, I, Satan, to distinguish him from You!"

That is, I upheld the Law You set forth. I will not adore Your creature separately from You, nor in fact Your creatures at all in You.

"I serve Him more purely (thus)..."

"So, by His truth, no, I have not sinned with regard to His decree; I have not challenged destiny! And I am not disturbed by the distortion of my form. I preserve my balance through these maxims. Were He to punish me with His fire for all eternity, I would not bow down before anyone... My declaration is that of sincere people. I myself am sincere in love!"

(Cf. *Akhbâr* 59: "There is no public declaration of love that doesn't conceal a lack of propriety.")

Hallaj himself bowed down before questionable and corrupt authorities in his final acceptance of martyrdom in order to draw the Community together against him and, in this sense, against that satanic self that retained a measure of separateness from God.

"How could I humble myself before Adam, You created me of fire and him of earth; those two opposites cannot be reconciled. And furthermore, I have served You for a longer time, I have a higher virtue, a vaster knowledge, and a more perfect (contemplative) function."

> On the notion of Satan as a "martyr of love":
> "... reward me, Master, since I am desolate.
> ... the origin of my vocation was bitter.
> Let he who wishes to record it hear this
>   declaration of mine,
> Read it, and know that I am a martyr."

And then the end of his state of bitterness is described: "The spring from which he draws is a low-lying pool, sucked dry."

Hallaj extends his role of commentator beyond the *persona* of Satan to satanic spirituality among mystics in general: "Satan is more informed than (those most eloquent mystics who kept silent about him; that is, than those afraid to speak about the forbidden) on the matter of worship; he is closer than they to His Being; he has devoted himself more zealously to serve Him; he has kept more to his vow than they; he has drawn nearer than they to the Beloved."

Again, Hallaj's teaching that God gives humans His grace of closeness in the form of anguish, through their desire to risk even the forbidden to know and serve Him more fully. As a human being, however, he is paradoxical, whereas Satan remains doggedly consistent to himself (in "balance") through rejection of any incarnation in Adam based on the undecreed notion that God has given to such a man a secret of Himself, a unifying soul. Hallaj both risks violation of the *haram* and ultimately surrenders through complete acceptance of the Law. Satan upholds the Law without that anguish caused by violating it, which, in his mind, would be to bow down before (that is, to share in any way the experience of) God's creature. Paradox is the human, not the angelic, condition; for Satan there is bitterness, not anguish.

"Anguish from being blamed is so unknown to me, therefore do not blame me (for witnessing consistently Your Transcendent Truth)."

And finally, prior to his discussion in this remarkable work of God's nature, proof of existence, plan, and instruction of how to witness, Hallaj concludes that for all his devotion Satan "was muddled. He ceased to trust in God. He said "I am worth more than Adam." He remained on this side of the veil. "He wallowed in mud and embraced damnation (himself) for the eternity of eternities."

There are some memorable aphorisms at the end of the work, including the following:

"The sage is "he who sees"; and Wisdom, It, resides "in Him Who exists." The sage abides by his act of knowledge (*irfân*) and becomes thereby the act of knowledge itself; but Wisdom is beyond that, and its Object (God) even more so."

"Moreover, fables," such as he has just told in his dramatic dialogue with Satan, "are the concern of story tellers, and Wisdom the concern of (those to whom it is gratuitously given)."

"Civility fits public figures, as exorcism fits the possessed; remembrance appeals to those who grieve, forgetfulness to those who grow up wild."

"For the true God is the Real, and the created world is only creation; and there is no harm in that."

The Problem of Universalism

The last point indicates in Hallaj an acceptance beyond Satan's comprehension that creation doesn't diminish God. Giving another perspective, perhaps more "theologically correct", one of Hallaj's early teachers, 'Amr Makkî, remarked "The Creator does no harm to His creation."

In Hallaj, the crosser of the threshold into the forbidden knowledge of God through union in love, discovers a quality of God unknown to most of the dour and basically timid mystics of his time, that God as Truth or, as he says in this same work, "the dwelling place of truth," is also the source of irony and paradox and freedom of thought about such forbidden subjects as Satan, and ultimately the way to unveiling the mystery of the statement that God is the Lord of the worlds (*rabbi'l-'âlamîn*), and thus the inviter to an acceptance of the two creations' oneness in Him rather than the condemner of one in extreme deference to the other through obsessive preoccupation with nature's corruptibility. Hallaj's universality and "balance" is distinct from his Satan portrait's, in that his own is based on a decentering of himself rather than a retaining of himself, through a substitution and attachment (*mahabba*) of God's Self for his surrendered self, so that he then dwells only in Truth, not as a statement against falsehood, but as a spiritually desired state to which he has arrived in a series of foreshadowings in his heart up to the final place of union, beyond the final death of his self. The human condition vis-à-vis ultimate knowledge of itself, always elusive and beyond itself, is the recognition and acceptance first of contradiction: between strict and particular adherence and universalistic yearning and thought, and between a series of apparent opposites that one must perceive without being able to ultimately resolve. Through his own engagement with conflicting historical forces, past and present, and his relatively detached movement through a wide range of often contradictory social, religious, and ethnic and racial circles, he reflects in this and other works ascribed to him a deep knowledge of the human condition and a balanced acceptance of its choices. For him neither the bitter purist nor the speculative universalist path was possible. The former confronted him through his long imprisonment, the latter was his likely devil's advocate during his prior "mission" in the world.

IV

THE QUESTION OF UNIQUENESS

As indicated previously, Hallaj was not unique within Islamic mysticism in his desire to unite with God or in his teachings to that end. And though there are important distinctions in character and emphasis between the vividly remembered and the less commemorated of the individual mystics, especially regarding the degree of union possible and allowable within the bounds of Qur'anic Sacred Law, the common link throughout the tradition is not originality or innovation but continuity and solidarity. The starting and the ending point for mystics as for all adherents was and is the Qur'an. As Hallaj was reported to have insisted (see Rûzbihân Baqlî, *Sharh-i-shathiyât, Les Paradoxes des soufis,* ed. H. Corbin, Tehran and Paris, 1966, p. 265): "Whoever knows the Qur'an resides in the Resurrection." But the notion of mystics conceiving an extreme witness of *Tawhîd,* a Hallaj, for instance, is of course not stated or indicated in the Holy Book, nor is the idea of a tradition of mysticism as such and thus is held in suspicion by literalist guardians of the text of the Revelation as the tradition bursts forth and begins to unfold from late in the first Islamic century onward. The burst, as noted, comes recurringly from the inevitably ascetical impulse to reform the disunited Community whose governing principle and very basis of identity as Islamic is Unity: through internal purification which cannot be achieved by outward action and social criticism. Asceticism of the heart within oneself was therefore the first step in the progress of the soul's witnessing of the essential unity of God revealed and taught in the Qur'an. It was not an individualistic path in its original conception nor in the teaching of Hallaj. Behavioral differences aside, such a notion was outside the thought of the early mystics of Islam, whether in Khurasan or Iraq. The model for the strict sublimation of self in service to the Qur'an was of course the Prophet Muhammad, who is therefore the rightful first witness of a mystical path conceived in the minds of all subsequent "mystics", including Hallaj despite his regarding the Prophet as having shied away from witnessing prematurely God's lifting of the veil between Himself and His creatures thereby delaying the coming of the Judgement (*in Tawâsîn*). From the Prophet onward thus, in Hallaj's thought, the ascetical mystics were continuing "witnesses" (*shawâhid*), including himself in the series, through time. This was characteristic of the tradition in the general sense among those who practised the so-called *'ilm al-qulûb*, the "science of hearts", apart from the *abdâl*, the "substitute saints" specially chosen to expiate through suffering for the whole Community, one of whom Louis Massignon in his many studies of Hallaj believed him to be. This latter subject remains controversial among both Muslim and Western scholars continuing to argue on the exegetical plane, with Massignon's textual erudition the starting point of the discussion, one that is beyond the limits of this study. Suffice it to say for our purposes that Hallaj in his time, given the prior and continuing development of strong Qur'anic based so-called "orthodox" schools of Law solidly resistant to Mu'tazilite speculative thought, did not veer far in the substance of his "mission"'s teaching from the fundamentals of his faith. His writings do not reveal an original message, but rather a person extending the message through very narrow limits of analogical thinking and unprofane metaphoric evocations to communicate freely and openly among adherents yearning for the Reality he embraced in moments beyond the veil. This was preaching and experience beyond the manuals, the established lexicon of the school mystics, the competence of the law to judge, and the right of any individual, not to witness, but to reveal. In reviewing 'Attâr's *tadhkirat* collection of the lives and emphases of the mystics, including Hallaj, who was given the longest notice, one finds the consistent call for the practise of voluntary poverty, further inward asceticism and privation, and *tawakkul* or trust in God alone: all internalizing the essential message closer and closer to the unveiling, the *kashf*, and the experience of embracing the One. Hallaj's fatal "originality" was that as an "orthodox" and extremely pious Muslim he "revealed," an indiscretion reserved to heterodox Mahdists, crackpots, and madmen feigning or real.

Another extreme lover of God to recall here was the previously cited Dhu'l-Nûn (245/859), on whose forehead at his death was written, according to Hujwîrî's *Kashf al-mahjûb*, the earliest biographical manual of mysticism in New Persian (Hujwîrî, d. 466/1072), "This is the friend of God, who died in love of God, killed by God." (H. 100) Hujwiri records the tradition that Dhû'l-Nûn set forth the notion of gnosis (*ma'rifa*), mystical knowledge of God beyond deductive learning. Scholars see in him the fusion of neo-Platonist and Qur'anic formulations alluded to before and apparent in Hallaj (note: E.G. Browne, H. Corbin, L. Massignon, S.N. Nasr, AM Schimmel, et al). Also cited previously and noteworthy to recall is the Persian Bâyezîd Bistâmî, whose *shathîyât* or "conversations with God" foreshadowed those of Hallaj and aroused the interest of the sober head of the Baghdad school, Junayd. Though some scholars have seen Hindu influences on Bâyezîd, AM Schimmel has concluded that he "reached his goal by means of the Islamic experience of *fanâ'*, annihilation, as he formulated it for the first time, rather than by an experience that, in the Vedantic sense, would have led him to an extension of the *atman*, "the innermost self". (*Myst. Dim. of Islam*, pp. 47-48) Bâyezîd, though he may like other Muslim mystics reflect comparative or corresponding formulations current in the third/ninth-fourth/tenth centuries in the schools of Khurasan and Baghdad and their satellites, defined extinction of the self more totally, in what would become the Hallajan vein, to the point of saying *Subhânî* or Praise to Me, meaning God in me, as his *shath* reveals, or "I am God," the mingling and confusion of lover with Beloved in love, which anticipates Hallaj's realization.

These principal ideas of Hallaj, ones which became associated in both the popular and the more critically denouncing mind with him alone, were thus expressed and experienced at least in potential by others as common property, so to speak, and by common blending or synthesis from a Qur'anic revelation setting the spiritual fact that when "He loves them, they love Him" ('Attâr 1:67 quoting Q 5:59) and when one knows God, one "knows God by God" (Sarrâj, d. 377/987, *K. al-luma'*, ed. R.A. Nicholson, 19). Both reveal God's prior inspiration of human response in love, the essential step to the mystic's decentering of self and recentering in God. While the degree and depth of influence from neo-Hellenistic or from Hindu philosophy upon these early mystics is challenging to ascertain, and the Qur'anic basis of their original inspiration and the object of their devotion is clearly defined in all of the manuals and collections of lives (Hujwîrî, 'Attâr, Sarrâj, Sulamî, d. 412/1021, et al) for obvious apologetical reasons, the question of a given mystic's uniqueness is very remote from Islamic consciousness and from the goal of mysticism itself. And synthesis does not constitute originality but one of the commonest recurring themes in both Islamic history and mysticism.

The point here is to identify Hallaj as part of highly developed and systematically presented mystical tradition in Islam, and to try to know him as part of a collective Muslim consciousness, universalistic in the Abrahamic monotheistic sense, adhering and responsive to the traditionalist conception of Sacred Law and ritual devotion. The very notion of one's being unique or original belonged to the self and its illusions to be annihilated through union with God the Unique One singled in Himself. This understanding of

God's Self was the result of Qur'anic revelation and centuries of ever deepening interior meditation on that revelation, even unto the Hallajian risk.

Here follows a number of expressions of union with God attributed to Hallaj in his most characteristic vein of spare, direct ecstatic utterance or narrative account of mystical love:

Akhbâr 3: "And You became the personal consciousness within my inmost self."

Qur'an 72:22 as quoted *Akhbâr* 10:" "No one can save me from God," for He has ravished me in myself and doesn't return me to who I am;"... nor have I any refuge but Him. " "

Ibid.; "And there is no moment given me when He veils Himself from my glances to give me some relief; and this even to the point of annihilating my humanity in His divinity, to the disappearance of my body in the light of His essence..."

Ibid.: "On the one hand, I feel no power to affirm the respect due to this Presence; on the other, I tremble for fear of being abandoned and becoming forsaken and cast away. Unfortunate is whosoever finds himself forsaken after knowing such a Presence and abandoned after such a union."

Akhbâr 1: When Husayn ibn Mansur was led out to be crucified, he looked up at the gibbet and at the nails and laughed so loudly that tears poured from his eyes...

"O my God ! You who appear to me on all sides but do not veil my side, I call to You in trust that You will bring forth my due and in trust that I bring forth Your due."

Akhbâr 11: "I find it strange that the Divine Whole can be borne by my little human part,

Yet due to my little part's burden the earth cannot sustain me.

If such a simple piece of land could be a place of calm repose,

I'm sure my heart, alas, before such a repose in men would be filled with anxiety.

Akhbâr 12: "Only the state of madness permits me to proclaim You Holy."

Akhbâr 30: "The attainment of union is both abyss and joy, and the ensuing separation both release and destruction. One swings back and forth between two inspirations, one clinging to the veils of Timelessness, the other foundering in the sea of nothingness."

Akhbâr 36: "O people! When *al-Haqq* (God) takes possession of a heart, He empties it of all else but Himself; and when He keeps a man for Himself, He ruins him for all else but Himself. When He lovingly desires a servant, He incites His other servants to enmity against him, so as to bring him closer to Himself."

Dîwân (ed. L.M., *Journal Asiatique,* Paris, 1931) *Muqatta'ât* no. 4, 1.4: "And even if, in the shadow, abandonment seizes you, move out into the light of the heart's peace."

Ibid, M. 6 (to his friend and disciple Ibn 'Atâ', who like Nûrî believed the way to union with God was through fraternal love): "I have written you, without writing you, for I have written to my Spirit (*Rûh*), without drafting a letter. To the Spirit, nothing can separate Him from those who love Him... There is no separation between lovers, and so the letter is sent."

Ibid., M. 10: "I have seen my Lord (*rabbî*) with the eye of my heart, and I said: who are You. He said: You."

(This most characteristic expression: *ra'aytu rabbî bi 'ayni qalbi fa qultu man anta qâlâ anta*)

Ibid., M. 15-16: "I have tried to be patient, but how can I be when my heart is deprived of my center?

Your Spirit is mixed with my spirit in drawing near and in separation;

And now I am You. Your existence is mine, and this is my wish (*murâdi*)."

Ibid., M. 17, 1.2: "The reality of God (*al-Haqq*) is far beyond. The fate of one who sees the reality of God is (far beyond); and the one who seeks it is anguished."

Ibid., M. 18, 1.1: "It is You who drives me mad with love, not my remembrance (in prayer) of You."

Ibid., M. 19: "As for the ecstatic states of *al-Haqq*, it is *al-Haqq* who causes all of them, whatever the wisdom of the masters leads them by way of self-renunciation to think."

Ibid., M. 21, 1.2 (partial): "... the breath of the Spirit breathes in my skin, my thought..."

Ibid., M. 24, 1.1: "Love as long it is hidden feels in danger, and it gains confidence only when it faces (danger)."

Ibid., M 30, 1.1-3: "You have shown so much of Yourself that it seems there is only You in me.

I return my heart to those who are not You,

but I see between us only strangeness and familiarity between You and me.

Alas, here I am, in the prison of life, surrounded by all men;

snatch me to Yourself away from my prison."

Ibid., M. 31, 1.5: "If I could go to You, I would arrive crawling on my face or walking on my head."

Ibid., M. 32, 1.3: "His Spirit is my spirit, and my spirit is His Spirit; what He wants, I want; and what I want, He wants."

Ibid., M. 34, 1. 1-3: "I do not cease swimming in the seas of love, rising with the wave, then descending; now the wave sustains me, and then I sink beneath it; love bears me away where there is no longer any shore."

Ibid., M. 35, 1.1: "Your place in my heart is my entire heart, nothing else has any place."

*Ibid., M.*41, 1.2: "One touches You, touches me."

Ibid., M. 43, 1.2: "I have a heart which has eyes open to You and to all that is in Your hand."

The drama of Hallaj could be seen as a *liebesdod* of the lover dying in the embrace of the Beloved, but for the fact that his love is not eternalized through the tragic yearning of a broken heart, but is a forestaste of a resurrection he has witnessed already with his Beloved "in solitudes (where He is) present though He is concealed. "(*Dîwân*, M. 11)

Resigned to death, believing profoundly in the resurrection, Hallaj wrote the following ode (*Dîwân*, ed. L.M.., pp. 31-35; ed. K.M. ash-Shaibi, Baghdad, 1974, no. 14), which proposes the thesis of *tadmîn*, germinal burial from which springs one's resurrection:

> So kill me now, my faithful friends
> For in my killing is my life.
> My death would be to live,
> My life would be to die.
> To me removal of my self
> Would be the noblest gift to give
> And my survival in my flesh
> The ugliest offense, because
> My life has tired out my soul
> Among its fading artifacts.
> So kill me, set aflame

My dried out bones,
And when you pass by my remains
In their deserted grave,
You will perceive the secret of my Friend
In the inmost folds of what survives.

One moment I'm a shaykh
Who holds the highest rank,
And then I am a little child
Dependent on a nurse

Or sleeping in a box
Within the brackish earth.

My mother gave her father birth,
Which was a marvel I perceived,
And my own daughters whom I made
Became my sisters in this way to me,
Not in the world of time
Nor through adulteries.

So gather all the parts together
Of the glowing forms
Or air and fire
And pure water

And sow them in unwatered soil;
Then water it from cups
Of serving maids
And flowing rivulets;

And then, when seven days have passed,
A perfect plant will grow.

V

REPRISE

WHO WAS HALLAJ AND WHAT IS HIS PLACE IN ISLAMIC MYSTICISM?

A. Who was Hallaj?

Born in 244/858 in SW Persia near a village called Bayda, the grandson of a Zoroastrian convert to Islam, the son of a *hallâj*, a man who earned his living as a woolcarder, a trade probably practised for a short time by Husayn ibn Mansûr "al-Hallâj" (the carder or reader of the secrets of the heart), a sobriquet he received from disciples met during his travels from Iraq through Iran and beyond to India, he was three times a pilgrim to Mecca; he wrote poetry and prose in Arabic of an intense direct spiritually experiential nature; he was monogamous and the father of three sons and a daughter.

He was trained as a child and early teenager in Hanbalite, strict Sunnite traditionalist, schools in SW Iran, from which he ventured to find spiritual teachers who could guide him to the more esoteric, inner meanings of the Qur'an than could or at least in his mind did his Hanbalite *kuttâb* teachers: first to Tustar, then into Iraq to Basra, and finally Baghdad, the great Muslim capital city, which he envisioned quite early as the site of his eventual confrontation with religious and secular authorities and of his martyrdom.

We know of him through histories of Baghdad, biographical polemics against or apologetical portraits for him, poets' collections, trial accounts, literary sketches, sayings attributed to him by his contemporary and later eyewitnesses or repeaters of events, ritual reenactments of his life, street songs, folk evocations, or, in modern literary retellings, in Turkey, Iran, India, Iraq, Lebanon and Egypt, through radio or stage plays or extended narrative poems. He was a historically verifiable person, the subject of a highly publicized trial, execution, and subsequent outburst of demonstrations in cities from Cairo to Baghdad to Bukhara and Samarqand.

He was born into an age of resurfacing "Hellenism" in the Near East, this time, moving from a declining Byzantium to an emerging Islam, in its new cultural, economic, and political center of Baghdad, ca. 813 AD, through the patronage of a new universalistically-minded Caliph, the son of the fabled Hârûn ar-Rashîd, al-Ma'mûn, who enriched the incipient Iranian and Greek learning translation center, *Bayt al-hikma*, instituted by his father, to make it the highlighted instrument for diffusing Greek analytic methods of inquiry and cultural manners and style and to position it as a beacon of quasi-legitimacy against the Qur'anic based traditionalism preached by the '*ulamâ*' entrenched in Islam since the death of the Prophet in 632 AD. A new school of thinkers, the so-called *failasûf*, questioned the literal readings of the Qur'an, pushing its possible metaphoric interpretations, and thus becoming in effect a rival intellectual elite in the major cities of Islam. The instituting of a *mihna* or inquisitional court by Ma'mûn further intensified the atmosphere of dogmatic rivalries leading even to the enforced proclamations of testaments of faith pro or contra the neo-Hellenists or, as they were called, the separatists, the Mu'tazilites, who enjoyed for his tenure the protection of Caliphal authority. The notion of "orthodoxy" was reversed after the death of Ma'mûn in 833 AD, and the traditionalists were once again or still the established authority, and speculative philosophers the marginal questioners.

The traditionalists had several major concerns, principally the affirmation of the Qur'an as a divine (not a Hellenistic cultural) source (cf. the more separated modern liberal education inclusion of the Bible as literature?); the guarding of the sacred through pious ritual observance of the precepts of the Law; their own authoritative representation of the Community, the so-called *ijma'* or consensus factor, in all matters of Sacred Law and religious obligation; and the witnessing of *Tawhîd* against sectarian disunity. Theirs was a religious and political affirmation; the two were inseparable in their minds, and remain so in extreme Sunnite and Shi'ite thinking despite different concepts of leadership election and elitism, exoteric and esoteric readings of the sources, to this day. In the traditionalists' view the Mu'tazila were dividers of the Community, relativists, "detached" analysts, separatists, comparatists, not obedient practitioners of the faith. They were in effect lackeys of foreign ideas and influences; their view of traditionalists was equally biased: against pedants, intractable literalists, conformist not imaginative thinkers, etc. The world into which Hallaj was born, intellectually speaking, was a world of cross-currents destined repeatedly for dramatic convergences.

Hallaj himself was seen by some as a representative of both, practising the ritual devotions watched over by the one, yet at ease and thus suspect by the one in the language and thought of the other. He moved freely in virtually all circles, was recognized early as a serious spiritual personality, was widely travelled, was considered "radical" from the time of his youth when he demonstrated against the Caliphal authorities on behalf of the Zanj salt field laborers condemned in southern Iraq o subhuman living conditions and slave labour, a position he repeated on behalf of starving Bedouins who stormed Basra and Baghdad desperate for food; and to the end his life, he raised the outcry to God, the Truth, the Just, on behalf of sufferers from injustice. His life, in this respect, was a consistent line, leading to his trial and execution.

His supporters came from high and low stations in life, as did his antagonists. Traditionalists for the most part, especially Hanbalites, supported him as a true practitioner of the faith; the philosophers, save those in Iran, opposed him. The major issue in the political arena of Baghdad that led to his major issue in the political arena of Baghdad that led to his trial and execution was his threat to law and public order, meaning to the Caliph's always fragile legitimacy and the power elites' monopoly of public resources and funds, both issues that raised the recurring question of authority and challenged presumptive officials' behavior, from both a traditionalist Sunnite and a Shi'ite point of view.

In the minds of his followers, Hallaj stood as a witness thus for the Community unity, the unity of ritual, the unity of the sacred, and the Oneness of God.

B. What is his place in Islamic mysticism?

Basing himself on a premise given by Ghazâlî (d. 505/1111), Louis Massignon explained (*Test. & Refl.*, NDU Press, 1989, p. 123) "that the study of mysticism is not like the study of other disciplines such as law, philosophy, and theology, in which it is sufficient to absorb through hypothesis the fundamental axioms in order to reconstruct and even extend the rational deductions implied in their premises. To understand mysticism one must have experienced, and willingly, the trials and sufferings of the most humble life. Junayd had said forcefully "we have not learned this science (of mysticism) by means of 'it is said' (*qîl wa qâl*), but by privations and separations from dear ones": applied asceticism.

"It is this initiation in "mental scouring" which is the axiom, not theoretical but practical, of mysticism."

In the case of Hallaj, the subject of his major study (*Passion*), the participation in suffering, in compassion unto substitution, the mystic "offers his life, turned toward the *qibla* of Mecca for the annual pardon of the Islamic Community: as a "present witness", here and now, of "the Eternal Witness." (*ibid*, p. 128)

In the "school of mystics" there is a language and a method of progressive states of soul and stage of ascent to be experienced. In this sense,

Reprise 81

mysticism is a science. The anagogic lexicon is Qur'anic in its source even if developed by synthetic fusing with "foreign" philosophy; the mystical words are germs of faith and renewal to be acted upon, not treated as abstractions or objects of casual reflection.

Ghazâlî's *ihyâ'* theme, like Hallaj's earlier testimony in blood, results not from philosophical speculation thus, but from first-hand experience, a lived path. This is the "given" in placing Hallaj in the tradition. Certain key ideas, though not unique to him, were given special authenticity by him through his ultimate experience or self-surrender, beginning and ending with the present witness of the Eternal Witness, *shâhid ânî*: initiated through desire to be one with God the Essential Desire (*'ishq dhâtî*) in a state of perfect unification in which one no longer remembers one's own name, *'ayn al-jam'*, when Divine Nature (*lâhût*) mingles with human nature (*nâsût*) in esctasy (*wajd*) of an informing and transforming moment (*waqt*), that spiritual interruption in our ordinary seemingly progressive or our circular time when the Divine point of unity, the *Tawhîd*, is revealed and perceived.

One is possessed by, unable to be freed from, God (*istilâm*) ; the heart (*qalb*) is attached to God alone (*i'tiqâd*) in the ideal union of two souls (*ittihâd an-nafsayn*), thus ending painful indeed agonizing separation (*firâq*): through the power of love (*hubb*) with the beloved (*Habîb*). In that power of union with the real, one can say *anâ'l-Haqq* without trace of ego or presumption: His individual and unique existence, *Huwa Huwa*, is my existence, *anî*, in a complete realization, *haqîqa*, of oneness, *wahdat ash-shuhûd*, known in witnessing.

After such union, with its series of raptures, there is a natural if melancholy spiritual exhaustion, requiring a convalescence (*barâ'an*): "I wish for my person a convalescence from Your love" (*Arjû li-nafsi barâ'an min mahabbikum*).

He entered the states of *zuhd* and *sabr* in the time honored ascetical spirit of Hasan of Basra, *tawakkul* or abandonment and complete trust in God in the manner of one of his spiritual guides Muhâsibî, and *mahabba* with the yearning, *shawq*, for intimacy of God of Râbi'a, to mention only the near archetypal figures of early Sufism. The classic exponents of the intoxication, *sukr*, state in the practise of mystical love, as mentioned earlier, were Bâyezîd, Nûrî, and the Egyptian Dhû'l-Nûn.

The "science of hearts" theme, the *'ilm al-qulûb*, had been developed earlier by one of the first to teach mystical states and stages, *ahwâl wa maqamât*, the maternal uncle of Junayd, Sarî' as-Saqatî (d. 253/867), a disciple of Muhâsibî quoted by Hujwîrî (RAN, *Kashf*, p. 111) as saying "Love is the vision of Him in hearts;" and like Muhâsibî and

Reprise

Junayd in that sequence down to Hallaj, he believed in the knowledge of the secrets of the heart's motions (*al-'ilm biharakat al-qulûb*). Hallaj's constant reference to "the heart" was an established term for the self's center, my center = *fawâdî*, the place touched most deeply, indeed wounded, by love, causing heart sickness, fear, anxiety.

Hallaj's positions on fundamentals of Islamic teaching were traditional and differed little if at all from other shaykhs of the time. His disagreements with his early teachers, 'Amr Makkî and Sahl Tustarî, were not due to attitudes of praxis or asceticism or obedience to Law, but, according to Hujwiri, to a kind of impulsiveness and sense of personal calling and need of disengagement from control by the older shaykhs, which led him to "leave without asking permission," in each case; and eventually led him to reject any long term association with established Sufism.

Two notes on Sahl and 'Amr Makkî: Sahl, directed spiritually for a time by Dhû'l-Nûn Mîsrî, was anti-neo-Hellenist, anti-Mu'tazilite, strongly traditionalist, who believed in submission to the State, and in the Qur'an as the primary recourse and balancer of mystics; a rigid adherent to form and discipline.

'Amr Makkî initiated Hallaj into Sufism, gave the *khirqa* and clipped his moustaches; a traditionlist pupil of Bukharī, the "sound" traditions compiler along with Muslim; an allegorist author, he also wrote on Satan but from the standpoint of the basic refusal to bow down thesis, without any psychological interpretation. He regarded Hallaj as too oriented to direct and immediate knowledge of God to remain with either of them.

In the case of Junayd, the difference on the question of *Tawhîd* seems to be one of degree of self-sublimation, of *fanâ' wa baqâ'*, not of the experiential principle; and spiritual knowledge, *ma'rifa*, though tied in Junayd to observance, *'ibadât*, as with Sahl and Makkî, and obedience to God's command, *amr*, also included love and was verifiable *fi'l-qalb* in both. But *'ayn al-jam'* was a transforming action sanctifying one, in Hallaj, requiring the overt and total experience in order to escape the timidity that can compromise the heart's desire, a state he found paralyzing the advocates of sobriety, *sahw*.

Shiblî was closer still to Hallaj on the subject of love, according to Hujwîrî: "Love obliterates from the heart all but the Beloved." But we add Hallaj's special note from *Dîwân* M.17: "The realization of God is given to one who craves it in anguish."

In response to the seemingly outrageous expression *anâ'l-Haqq*, whether he actually uttered it or not, Jalâl ad-Dîn Rûmî, d. 672/1273, is to be considered as a voice in the controversy and dread that persist regarding Hallaj down to the present day: to say *anâ' l-Haqq* is much humbler than to say *'Abd Allâh*, for in the former there is no retaining of self to assert distinction, whereas in the latter one affirms oneself as separate indeed pretentiously as a servant.

Perhaps sophistry, but nevertheless spoken fraternally of one lover of God by another.

The place of Hallaj in Islamic mysticism is assured by the ongoing controversy surrounding his execution and fueled by any revival of interest whether pro or con. His martyrdom seems frozen in time yet is thawed, so to speak, by any retelling be it by poets or dogmatists. To some semi-supporters he was a truly pious man who went too far; to enthusiasts he was a sincere triumphant lover of God; to modern "fundamentalists" in parts of the Arab world, Pakistan, etc., he was a heretic who deserved to die as he did; to liberal secularists, if they know of him at all, he was a social reformer way ahead of his time. The research and published studies of the late Professor Louis Massignon (d. 1962) of the Collège de France add enormous dignity and prestige to any consideration of Hallaj. Indeed, in order to approach this figure, his life and times, his civilization, his death, and his legacy, one has to begin with the body of

Massignon's major and minor works. It is a unique factor in the history of Western orientalism, and is based heavily on the immense erudition of this modern French scholar, but even more on his own personal presence and aura of piety, which, in its Catholic Christian form, carried him to a profound sense of correspondence, beyond academic study, with the Muslim mystical tradition in general and with Hallaj in particular. Further, many distinguished Muslim scholars and writers see in Massignon an Abrahamic co-religionist and a major contributer to world understanding and appreciation of their civilization. To seriously denounce Hallaj in order to rid the civilization of an apparent scandal, one that God Himself could not possibly have allowed to happen, one must chip away at Massignon's research, which has of course begun in certain circles and from different motives and perspectives: all of which adds to keeping Hallaj "alive". This is a separate literature in itself, however, and far from the range and purpose of this present brief review.

Many scholars, Muslim and Western, include Hallaj in their own studies of Islamic mysticism, with due acknowledgment given to the work of Massignon. Prior to this work, begun in 1907 and completed with the posthumous publication of his *Passion d'al-Hallaj* in 1975 in its enlarged second edition, Hallaj was virtually unknown though included in most manuals and memorials of Sufism within the Muslim world. It is not an exaggeration to say that Hallaj through Massignon was instrumental in communicating the universal quality of Islamic mysticism to those outside his civilization. And this quality continues to enlarge its range of admirers and adherents in our time.

VI

The following are personal evocations of Hallaj, his disciples, and his martyrdom, included here merely as one further response to his presence. They are reprinted with permission of Notre Dame University Press, Indiana, and the journal SUFI of London.

AFTER HALLAJ

"If you are seized
    by the shadow,
Step out into the light
    of the heart's peace."*

If you are lost
    and wonder who you are,
Listen as the Beloved
    Tells you: I am you.

You will forget your name
    and where you're from;
You will know only
    you are no one, found

Not by someone who

       will boast and count
The many rescues
       he has made.

But by the Only One
       who tells you nothing
And guides in hiddenness
       to His source of Love.

A blood rose may be thrown
       by someone at your heart:
An emblem of your now-
       forgotten separation.

       *from Hallaj's *Dīwān*, M.4, 1.4

SHIBLI*

You have heard
That I remained
Beneath the cupola of poets
Or in the zawiya of saints.

In fact, I was afraid
Of being put with either;

And that is why I feigned
With bursts of rhetoric and song
My half-wit acts of joy and pain,
And let myself be put away
Inside the maristan.

I was afraid of being merely all
Alone with my beloved One,

Like someone else. I was afraid
Of dying young or old. And that is why
I threw a rose when he was on his cross
Performing his ablution in his blood.

Ours were the acts of lovers
Mad with love.
Only my madness saved me,
While his reason brought him death.

*from Hujwîrî, *Kashf*

THE DEATH OF AL - HALLAJ *

HALLAJ
You know, my friend, our surgeons prove to us
That our hearts have two chambers that contain
A mixture of blood and living breath.
They are analogous to the spirit and reason,
To divine inspiration and human expiration.
He gives us consciousness within our heart,
And *we* become with Him the One Who gives us life.
I was a corpse He reclothed as a body.
We each are His epiphanies, we see
In each of us the presence He has made;
The action He has given us, the life.
His whole creation is aglow with life.
And we respond to it through what's alive
In us. I was in ecstasy last night
Embracing and embraced by Him, as one

Small residue of life. When I am gone
I know He'll breathe into my heart again.

    (Pauses)

Let us rest from words.

    IBN ATA

No, master, I cannot let you stop.

There isn't time.

(from pp. 37-38)

    HALLAJ

Immersion is what God requires of us,
Not prudence or restraint. He is the sea
And signals us to lose ourselves in Him.
We are poor swimmers and the undertow
Is frightening, but the water's edge
Attracts us breathless. We go to the sea
To draw its steady breathing, like the
Camel at the well, to replenish ourselves.
We must conquer our fear, we must plunge much
Deeper, for God is deeper than water.

(from pp. 56-57)

    IBN ATA

Will I see you again, master?

    HALLAJ

Yes, when I am on the esplanade.
We may not have a chance to speak,
But don't be afraid nor try to join me.

The Death of Al-Hallaj

For your way is yours, don't imitate mine.
You'll find your way.

> IBN ATA

When, master?

> HALLAJ

When in a crowd or alone you perceive
Impatience disappearing, and you know
Just where you are and where
You're meant to be.

> IBN ATA

Where is that, master?

> HALLAJ

Anywhere. You will know your action.
You are present there, not thinking of some-
Where else you ought to be.

> IBN ATA

I am afraid without you, master,
Not hearing your words.
Can you bequeath me a maxim
To hold and live by in your absence?

> HALLAJ

Only to subdue yourself or yourself
Will subdue you. I am not afraid for you,
And don't be afraid of being labelled strange.
There is a freedom in strangeness.

Exposure frees us from anxiety.
You must leave now.
The jailor is upset by long farewells.

(from pp. 58-60)

HAMD NARRATING

On the morning of the execution
He was taken from his prison,
Put on one of the pack mules,
Led away, jostled by grooms
Who ran alongside him
Shouting at the crowd which formed
A mob. The commissioner,
Afraid himself of being killed
Or of someone killing his prisoner,
Said: "This is not Hallaj,
Hallaj is in the Palace of Vizirs."
While Hamid's mounted guard
Escorted him, the commissioner,
To the esplanade, near the Khurasani
Gate, on the West Bank of the Tigris
Where the gibbet was set up.
Everyone who lived in Baghdad
And hundreds of foreign visitors
To the City of Peace were there.
Never had such a crowd formed
To witness an execution.
The guards lifted him from the mule
And he began dancing in his chains.

The Death of Al-Hallaj

The guards were shocked, the people
Who could see burst into nervous laughter,
And then they led him to the gibbet.
They tore the clothes from his back
And began the ordered flagellation.
"Now Constantinopole is taken!" he shouted,
At the five hundredth lash. He fainted
And the commissioner ordered
The flagellation stopped
Lest he die without suffering
The full prescribed punishment.
The guards had been ordered to close their ears
Lest they be seduced to show him mercy.
Once the lashes had been stopped
The executioner cut off one of his hands
And then a foot, and then the other hand
Followed as prescribed by the other foot.
He then was hoisted on the gibbet in display.
The air was filled with screams.
The commissioner ordered the decapitation
Postponed until the morning
So the vizir, Hamid, could be present.
That night his friends and enemies
Came to him, challenging him
To answer for himself. Looters
Roamed the city, setting fire to shops.
Baghdad was convulsed with rioting.
He cried out to God: "O my Friend, my Friend...."
His disciples came... and said

To the gibbet: "Have we not forbidden you
To receive a guest, neither angel nor man!"
One threw a rose at my father,
Who raised his bloody stump
And wiped his cheek
Where it had struck him.
Life ebbed from him
And he could barely speak.
In the morning Hamid came.
He had ordered the official witnesses
At the trial scattered through the crowd
To cry out: "This is for the salvation
Of Islam. Let his blood fall on our necks!"
Advancing toward the gibbet Hamid drew
From his sleeve a scroll which he handed
To the commissioner to unroll.
The latter handed it back to him. It had
The names of eighty-four learned men on it,
The legal scholars and Koran reciters,
Attesting to his heresy. A placard
Was raised that later would be pinned
To his head, saying "this is the head
Of the blasphemous conniver and deceiver
Husayn Ibn Mansur al-Hallaj,
One whom God has put to death
At the hands of Caliph al-Muqtadir
After proof was given showing that he claimed
The sovereignty of God himself.
Glory be to God, who causes his blood

The Death of Al-Hallaj

To be shed and led him to be cursed."
The crowd shouted: God is great!
Hamid then called for the witnesses
To reenact the trial, as was prescribed,
Arguing the pros and cons and finally
Concurring with the statement read.
Hamid then asked: "The Caliph is innocent
Of his blood?" They shouted "Yes!"
"The commissioner is innocent of his blood?"
"Yes. Let his blood fall on our necks!"
Then Hamid returned the scroll to his sleeve
And lowered his right hand. The executioner
Stepped forward and the guards took
My father down. As he was being lowered
He cried out "the ecstatic
Wants only to be alone with his Only One."
The executioner beheaded him.
His body was wrapped in his mantle
And doused with oil and set aflame
Together with his books
The sellers had been ordered to bring forth.
One half-crazed disciple came forward
And pushed at the coals with his stick,
Saying to them "Speak!"
Some said "Like Jesus he could not die.
Another took his place."
And others said he stole the word God gave him
To keep in secret and used it to exalt himself.
And that is why he was put to death.

The ashes were taken up and thrown
From a minaret into the Tigris.
His head was carried to the Caliph's palace
Across the Tigris on the Bridge of Boats.
It was hung on a gate for everyone to see.
The walls of the palace behind him were high.
The power and majesty of what men build
Is awesome.

(from pp. 76-81)

*Excerpts from THE DEATH OF AL-HALLAJ

Notre Dame University Press, Indiana, 1979.

VII

SELECTED BIBLIOGRAPHY

'Abd al-Ṣabbūr, Salāḥ, *Ma'sāt al-Ḥallāj*. Cairo, 1966; Eng. tr. K.I. Semaan, *Murder in Baghdad*, Leiden, 1972.

Aktay, Salih Zeki. *Hallac-i Mansur*. Istanbul, 1942.

Anawati, G.C. and Gardet, L. *Mystique musulmane*. Paris, 1961.

Arberry, A.J. *Sufism*. London, 1950.

—— ed. *Muslim Saints and Mystics*, (from Aṭṭār's *Tadhkirat al-awliyā'*) London, 1964.

Arnaldez, Roger. *Hallaj ou la religion de la croix*. Paris, 1964.

'Aṭṭār, Farīduddīn. *The Conference of the Birds*, Tr. C.S. Noth, Berkeley, 1971.

Awn, Peter J. *Satan's Tragedy and Redemption: Iblis in Sufi Psychology*. Leiden, 1983.

Baghdādī, Abū Bakr ibn Thābit Khatīb al -. *Ta'rīkh Baghdād* excerpted *Quatre Textes*, L. Massignon.

Bayati, 'Abd al-Wahhāb. *Dīwān*,. 2 Vols. Beirut, 1972.

Chabbi, Jacqueline. "Reflections sur le soufisme iranien primitif," *Journal Asiatique*. 266 (1978).

Gardet, Louis. "Experience du Soi, Experience des profondeurs *de Dieu.*" Revue Thomiste 78 iii (1978)

Gardet, Louis, "Al-Ḥallādj", *Ency. of Islam*, new ed., Leiden-London, 1965.

Ghalib, Dr. Muṣṭafā. *Al-Ḥallāj.* Beirut, 1402/1982.

Guljān, 'Abbās. *Manṣūr-i Ḥallāj.* Tehran, 1354.

Hashmi, Hasan ud-Din. "Al-Hallaj Between Reality and Misunderstanding." *Jusur*, v.3 (1987).

Ḥallāj, Ḥusayn ibn Manṣūr al- *Dīwān*, ed. L. Massignon.
  Journal Asiatique, Paris, January-July 1931.
—— *Kitāb at-Ṭawāsīn*, text arabe, ed. L. Massignon, Paris, 1913.
—— *Kkhbār al-Ḥallāj*, ed. L. Massignon and Paul Kraus. 3rd ed. Paris, 1957.

Hujwīrī, 'Alī ibn 'Uthmān al- *Kashf al-maḥjūb , The Oldest Persian Treatise on Sufism.* Tr. R.A. Nicholson. Reprint London, 1959.

Iṣfahānī, Abū Nu'aym al. *Ḥilyat al-awliyā'*, 10 vols. Cairo, 1932-1939.

Kamran, Gilani. *Ana al-haqq Reconsidered.* Lahore, 1398/1977.

Kharṭabīl, Sāmī, *Usṭūrat al-Ḥallāj.* Beirut, 1979.

Lings, Martin. *What is Sufism?* London, 1983.

Mardam, Adnān. *al-Ḥallāj*, a play. Beirut, 1971.
Mason, Herbert. *The Death of al-Hallaj*. Notre Dame University Press, 1979.
Massignon, Louis. *The Passion of al-Hallaj*, (Vol. 4 extensive bibliography), Eng. tr. H. Mason. Princeton University Press, 1983; abridgement, Princeton, 1994.
—— *Quatre textes inédits relatifs à la biographie d'al-Hallaj.* Paris, 1914.
—— *Opéra Minora*, 3 vols, ed. Y. Moubarac. Beirut, 1962-63.
—— *Parole donnée*, ed. V. Monteil. Paris, 1962.
—— *Testimonies and Reflections*, ed. and tr. H. Mason, Notre Dame, 1989.
—— *Essay on the Technical Language of Muslim Mysticism*, Eng. tr. B. Clark, Notre Dame, 1995.
Nasr, Seyyed H. *Ideals and Realities of Islam.* London, 1966.
—— *Sufi Essays.* London, 1972.
Nwyia, Paul. *Exegèse coranique et langage mystique.* Beirut, 1970.

Reinert, B. "Gunaid und Hallāg's Iblīs" XXII. Deutscher Orientalistentag vom 21 bis 25. März 1983 in Tübingen.
Ritter, Hellmut. "Hasan al-Basrī, Studien sur Geschichte der islamischen Frömmigkeit," *Der Islam* 21 (1933).

Rūmī, Maulāna Jalāuddīn. *Mathnawi-i Ma'nawi*, ed. and tr. R.A. Nicholson, 8 vols. London 1925-40.

Saḥrāwī, 'Abd al-Qādir al- "al-Ḥusayn ibn Manṣūr al-Ḥallāj, "*Da'wat al-Haqq* 12, vi (May, 1969).

Sarrāj, Abū Naṣr as- *Kitāb al-luma' fī't-taṣawwuf*, ed. R.A. Nicholson. Leiden-London 1914

Schaeder, H.H. "Hasan al-Baṣrī" Der Islam 13 (1923).

Schimmel, A.M. *Al-Halladsch, Märtyrer der Gottesliebe.* Köln, 1979.

—— *As Through a Veil: Mystical Poetry in Islam.* New York, 1982.

—— "The Martyr-Mystic Ḥallāj in Sindhi Folk Poetry," *Numen* 9, no. 3 (1962).

—— *Mystical Dimensions of Islam.* North Carolina U. Press, 1975.

Schuon, F. *Le Soufisme, voile et quintessence.* Paris, 1980.

Shaibi, Kāmil M. ash. *Dīwān al-Ḥallāj*, edition Baghdad, 1974.

—— *al-Ḥallāj mauḍū'an li'l-adab wa'l-funūn al-'arabiyya wa'sh-shargiyya.* Baghdad, 1977.

—— *Sharh Dīwān al-Ḥallāj.* Baghdad, 1973.

Smith, Margaret, *Rābi'a the Mystic and Her Fellow Saints in Islam.* Cambridge, 1928.

—— *Readings from the Mystics of Islam.* London, 1950.

—— *The Sufi Path of Love.* London, 1954.

Sulami, "Abd ur-Rahmān as-*Kitāb tabaqāt aṣ-Ṣufiyya,*, ed. Nūraddin Sharība Cairo, 1953; ed. J. Pedersen. Leiden, 1960.

Surūr, Ṭāhā 'Abd al-Bāqī. *Al-Husayn ibn Manṣūr al-Ḥallāj, shahīd al-taṣawwuf al-islāmī.* Cairo, 1961.

Tadayyun 'Atā' Allāh. *Ḥallāj wa rāz-i Anā al-Haqq* Tehran, 1370/1992.

Tremaine, Louis. "Witnesses to the Event in *Ma'sat al-Ḥallāj* and *Murder in the Cathedral*, "*Muslim World* 62 (1977).

Watt. W.M. *Muslim Intellectual: a Study of Al-Ghazali.* Edinburgh, 1963.

NAME INDEX

'Alî ibn 'Isâ (d. 334/946), 20, 23, 25
'Attâr, Farîduddîn (d. 617/1220), 30, 46, 67-68
Bal 'amî, Abû'l-Fadl (d. 329/940), 24-25
Bâyezîd Bistâmî, Tayfûr ibn 'Isâ (d. 261/874), 36, 67, 82
Dhû'l-Nûn Misrî, Thaubân ibn Ibrâhîm (d. 245/859), 36, 66, 82-83
Ghazâlî, Abû Hâmid al- (d. 505/1111), 80-81
Hamd, son of Hallaj, 12, 23, 27, 31, 93
Hâmid, M. ibn al-'Abbâs (d. 311/923), 20-21, 23-27, 32, 93-96
Hanbalites, 20, 26, 49-50
Hasan of Basra (d. 110/728), 2-4, 7-8, 33, 41, 44
Hujwîrî, 'Alî ibn 'Uthmân (d. 464/1071), 66, 68, 82, 84, 90
Iblîs, Satan, 21-22, 55-61, 84
Ibn 'Arabî, Muhyîddîn M. (d. 638/1240), 51

Ibn 'Atâ', Abû'l-'Abbâs (d. 309/922), 26-27, 36, 90-92
Ibn Dâwûd, Abû Bakr M. (d. 297/909), 16, 18
Ibn Fâtik, Ibrâhîm (d. before 348/959), 29
Ibn Khaldûn, 'Abdû'r-Rahmân (d. 808/1406), 43-44
Ibn Surayj, Abû'l-'Abbâs Ahmad (d. 305/917), 16, 18, 20
Ibn Taymîya, Ahmad (d. 728/1328), x, 34, 50-53
Jesus, 11, 17
Junayd, Abû'l-Qâsim M. al- (d. 298/910), 3, 8, 35, 67, 82-84
Karnabâ'î, Hallaj's in-laws, 5, 9
al-Khadir, archetypal mystic guide, 11
The Mahdî, 6, 10, 20
Makkî, 'Amr ibn 'Uthmân (d. 297/909), 3, 8-9, 61, 83-84
Muhammad, Prophet (d. 11/632), 4, 53, 64
Muhâsibî, al-Hârith ibn Asad al- (d. 243/857), 3, 15, 82

al-Muqtadir, Caliph (re. 296/ 908-320/932), 19-20, 24-25
al-Mu'tadid, Caliph (re, 279/ 892-290/902), 14-15
Mu'tazilites, 10, 12, 48, 50, 65, 77-78, 83
Nûrî, Abû'l-Husayn an- (d. 295/907), 14, 36, 56, 82
Qarmathians, 10, 14, 21
Qushûrî, Nasr (d. 316/928), 23-27
Râbi'a al-'Adawiyya (d. 185/ 801), 15, 44, 82
Rûmî, Maulana Jalâluddîn (d. 672/1273), x, 46, 82
Saqatî, Sarî' as- (d 253/867), 82
Sarrâj, Abû Nasr as- (d. 378-988), 68
Shaghab, mother of Caliph at Muqtadir (d. 321/ 933), 18, 20, 24, 27
Shalmaghânî, Abû'l-Ja'far (d. 322/933), 33
Shiblî, Abû Bakr ibn Jahdar ash- (d. 334/945), 14, 31, 37, 89
Sulamî, Abû 'Abdu'r-Rahmân as- (d. 412/1021). 31, 68
Tabarî, Abû Ja'far M. ibn Jarîr (d. 310/923), 26
Tirmidhî, M. ibn 'Ali al-Hakîm (d. 321/932), 36
Tustarî, Ibn 'Abdallâh Sahl at- (d. 283/896), 2, 83-84
Zanj, 5, 7, 12, 18, 79

INDEX OF TERMS

abdâl, 15, 65
abnâ' ad-dunyâ, 9
akhbâr, ix-x, 69-72
anwârî thâtîhi, 1
'asabiyya, 44-45, 47
al-asrâr, al-qulûb, 12
'ayn al-jam', 81, 84

fanâ' wa baqâ', 41, 67, 84
fatwâ, 16, 20, 51-52
fawâdî, 83
firâq, 82

hajj, 33, 52
hallâj, al-Hallâj, xi-xii, 1, 12, 31, 36, 77
haqq, al-Haqq, haqîqa, Anâ'l-Haqq, 27, 33, 70-72, 82, 85

'ibâda, 55, 84
ilhâm, 8, 16, 36
'ilm al-qulûb, qalb, 12, 65, 81-84
infirâd, 22
'ishq dhâtî, 15, 81
istighrâq, 38
istilâm, 81
i'tiqâd, 81
ittihâd an-nafsayn, 81

kâfir, 17
al-kahf, 47

kashf, 65-66

khawf wa huzn, 8
khirqa, 84

Lâhût wa nâsût, 81

mahabba, hubb, Habîb, 15, 62, 82
ma'rifa, 'īrfân, 60, 66
mudda'î, 8
makr, 27

Rûh, ar-, 71

sabr, 82
sahw wa sukr, 36, 82, 84
sayha bi'l-Haqq, 7, 46
shâhid ânî, shawâhid, shuhûd, 16, 26, 64, 81-82
shath, shathîyât, 16, 46, 66-67
suliba, 31

tâ'a, 55
talâsha, 1
ta'rîf, 17
tawakkul, 66, 82
Tawâsîn, Tâ'Sîn al-Azal, xiii, 21, 23, 56-61, 64
Tawhîd, 52, 56, 63 78, 81, 84

'Umra, 7
'uyûb an-nafs, 29

wajd, 81
waqt, awqât, 22, 81

zandaqa, 15, 51